SCOTT FORESMAN · ADDISON WESLEY
Mathematics

Math Diagnosis and Intervention System

Booklet L

Statistics, Data Analysis, and Probability
in Grades 4–6

Overview of Math Diagnosis and Intervention System

The system can be used in a variety of situations:

- **During school** Use the system for intervention on prerequisite skills at the beginning of the year, the beginning of a chapter, or the beginning of a lesson. Use for intervention during the chapter when more is needed beyond the resources already provided for the lesson.

- **After-school, Saturday-school, summer-school (intersession) programs** Use the system for intervention offered in special programs. The booklets are also available as workbooks.

The system provides resources for:

- **Assessment** For each of Grades K–6, a Diagnostic Test is provided that assesses that grade. Use a test at the start of the year for entry-level assessment or anytime during the year as a summative evaluation.

- **Diagnosis** An item analysis identifies areas where intervention is needed.

- **Intervention** Booklets A–M identify specific topics and assign a number to each topic, for example, A12 or E10. For each topic, there is a page of Intervention Practice and a two-page Intervention Lesson that cover the same content taught in a lesson of the program.

- **Monitoring** The Teaching Guide provides both Individual Record Forms and Class Record Forms to monitor student progress.

PEARSON

Scott Foresman

Editorial Offices: Glenview, Illinois • Parsippany, New Jersey • New York, New York

Sales Offices: Needham, Massachusetts • Duluth, Georgia • Glenview, Illinois
Coppell, Texas • Ontario, California • Mesa, Arizona

ISBN: 0-328-07655-4

Copyright © Pearson Education, Inc.
All Rights Reserved. Printed in the United States of America. This publication or parts thereof, may be used with appropriate equipment to reproduce copies for classroom use only.

4 5 6 7 8 9 10 V084 12 11 10 09 08 07 06 05

Table of Contents

		Intervention Lesson Pages	Intervention Practice Pages	\multicolumn{4}{l}{The same content is taught in the Scott Foresman-Addison Wesley Mathematics Program}
Booklet L				Gr. 3	Gr. 4	Gr. 5	Gr. 6
\multicolumn{8}{l}{**Reading and Making Graphs**}
L1	Recording Data from a Survey	1	63	4-5			
L2	Reading and Making Pictographs	3	64	4-7, 4-11	4-6		
L3	Reading and Making a Bar Graph	5	65	4-12	4-7	5-2	11-5
L4	Graphing Ordered Pairs	7	66	4-9	4-9		
L5	Reading and Making Line Graphs	9	67	4-13, 4-10	4-10	5-3	11-6
L6	Choosing Appropriate Graphs	11	68		4-14	5-8	
L7	Circle Graphs	13	69		9-12	5-7	11-7
L8	Double Bar Graphs	15	70				11-5
L9	Scatterplots	17	71				11-6
\multicolumn{8}{l}{**Predictions and Probability**}
L10	Understanding Probability	19	72	12-7			
L11	Fair and Unfair	21	73	12-8			
L12	Finding Probability	23	74	12-9	12-7		
L13	Understanding Probability	25	75		12-5		
L14	Listing Outcomes	27	76		12-6		
L15	Displaying Probability Data and Making Predictions	29	77		12-8		
L16	Predictions and Probability	31	78			5-10	11-13
L17	Predicting Outcomes	33	79			5-11	
L18	Finding Probability	35	80			5-12	
L19	Counting Methods	37	81				11-10
L20	Permutations and Combinations	39	82				11-11
L21	Representing Probability	41	83				11-12
L22	Adding Probabilities	43	84				11-14
L23	Independent Events	45	85				11-15
L24	Dependent Events	47	86				11-15
\multicolumn{8}{l}{**Statistics**}
L25	Making Line Plots	49	87	4-6	4-7, 4-13	5-1	
L26	Mean, Median, and Mode	51	88		4-12	5-6	11-2
L27	Finding Averages	53	89		7-12		
L28	Stem-and-Leaf Plots	55	90			5-4	11-4
L29	Sampling Methods	57	91				11-1
L30	Frequency Tables and Line Plots	59	92				11-3
L31	Misleading Graphs	61	93				11-9

Name _____

Math Diagnosis and Intervention System

Intervention Lesson **L1**

Recording Data from a Survey

Example

Take a survey. First, write four activities on the chart.
Then ask classmates which activity they like best.
Tally the answers. Then write the total.

Activities

Activity	Tally	Total

1. Make a bar graph.
   Color one box for each time an activity was chosen.

   Activity

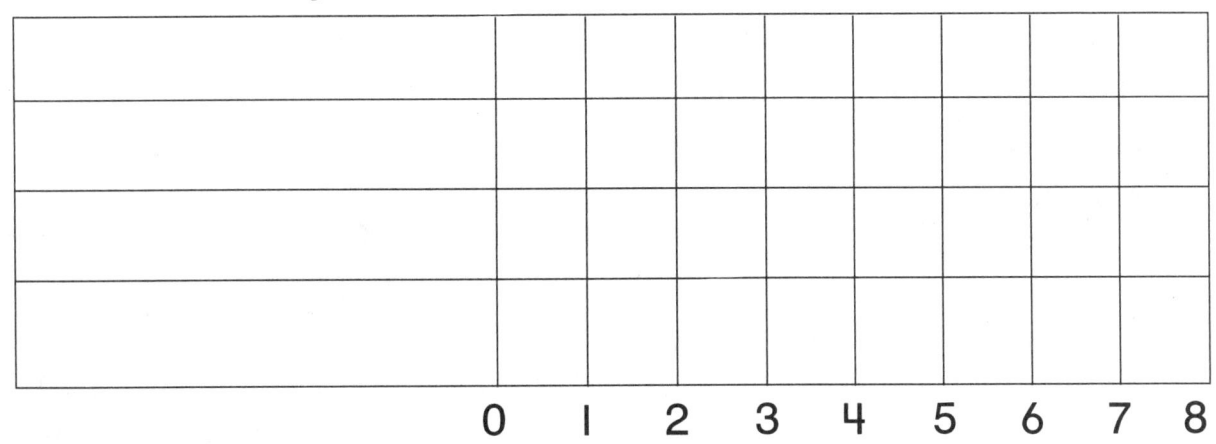

   0 1 2 3 4 5 6 7 8

Name _____

Math Diagnosis and Intervention System

Intervention Lesson **L1**

Recording Data from a Survey (continued)

Tallies are made in groups of 5. Count by 5s to get the number of tallies.

$\cancel{||||} \ || = 7$

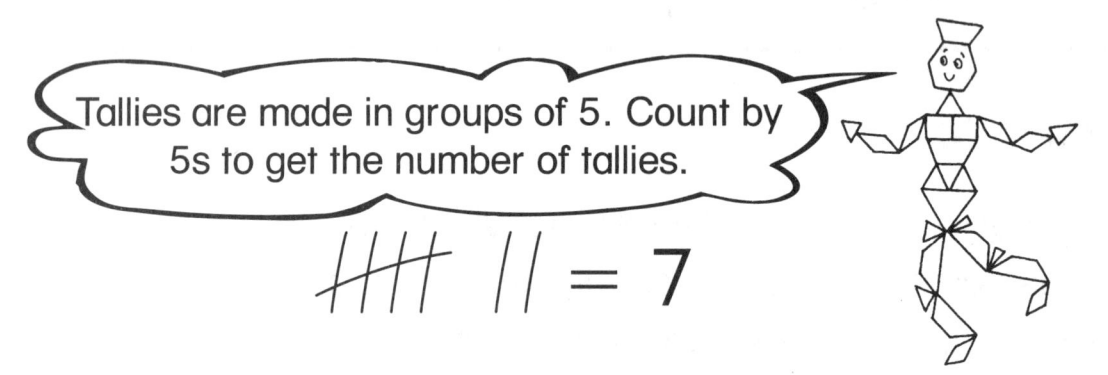

2. Andrea asks 10 classmates if they like football. She makes a tally mark to show each answer. Fill in the totals for those who like and dislike football.

Who Likes Football?

Answer	Tally	Total
Yes	$\cancel{||||}\ |$	
No	$||||$	

3. Make a bar graph to show how many children like football. Color one box for every child who likes football. Then use a different color and color one box for every child who does NOT like football.

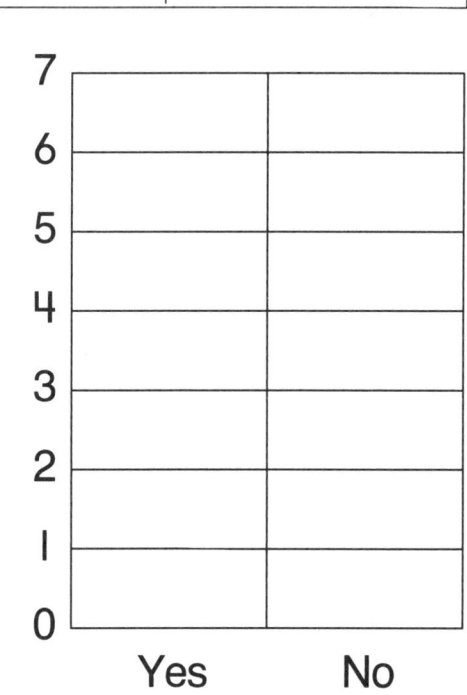

Name _____

Intervention Lesson **L2**

Reading and Making Pictographs

Example 1

Pictographs use pictures to show data.

The **key** explains what each picture represents.

Number of Fish in the Aquarium

Silver Molly	🐟 🐟 🐟 🐠
Black Neon Tetra	🐟 🐟 🐟 🐟 🐟
Angel Fish	🐟 🐠

Key: Each 🐟 = 2 fish. Each 🐠 = 1 fish.

How many Silver Molly are in the aquarium?
Use the key.
Think: Each 🐟 represents 2 fish.
Each 🐠 = 1 fish.
Count the 🐟 and the 🐠.

There are 3 🐟 and 1 🐠.
So, 2 + 2 + 2 + 1 = 7.
There are 7 Silver Molly fish in the aquarium.

Example 2

Use the data in the tally table to make a pictograph.

Favorite Pizza Toppings

Toppings	Tally	Number
Sausage	IIII	4
Vegetables	II	2
Pepperoni	IIII IIII	10

Favorite Pizza Toppings

Sausage	🍕 🍕
Vegetables	🍕
Pepperoni	

Key: Each 🍕 stands for 2 votes.

Step 1: Write a title to explain what the pictograph shows.

Step 2: Choose a symbol for the key. A small pizza is a good symbol. Decide how many votes each pizza will represent. Add this to the key.

Step 3: Draw the symbols that are needed for each topping.

Use the pictograph in Example 1 to answer Questions 1–2.

1. There are ___ Black Neon Tetra in the aquarium.

2. How many Silver Molly and Angel Fish are there in all? ___

3

Reading and Making Pictographs (continued)

3. Use the data in the table to make a pictograph.

Fruit Juice	
Lemonade	
Milk	

Favorite Drinks

Drinks	Tally	Number
Fruit Juice	|||| |||	8
Lemonade	|||| |||| ||	12
Milk	||||	4

Key: Each 🥛 stands for _____ votes.

4. What does each 🥛 on the graph represent?
_____

5. How many symbols did you draw for milk? ____ symbols

6. Which drink has 6 symbols? _____

7. Writing in Math Do any kinds of drinks on the pictograph have the same number of votes? How do you know?
_____
_____

8. Mental Math Use mental math to find how many votes were made in the survey. _____

Test Prep Circle the correct letter for the answer.

Use the pictograph in Question 3 to answer Questions 9–10.

9. How many more votes are there for lemonade than for milk?

   A 20   **B** 5   **C** 15   **D** 8

10. Which drink is the favorite?

   A Fruit Juice   **B** Lemonade   **C** Milk   **D** None

Name _____

Intervention Lesson **L3**

Reading and Making a Bar Graph

Example

Greta's class is voting on themes for class parties. Make a horizontal bar graph to display the data in the table:

First draw and label the side and the bottom of the graph. Use a scale that begins at 0 and goes beyond the highest number in the data. Draw bars on the graph that show the number of students who voted for each theme. Choose a title for your graph.

Theme	Tally	Number
Costume	IIII	4
The 1970s	ҴI	6
The Beach	Ҵ	5
The Future	Ҵ III	8

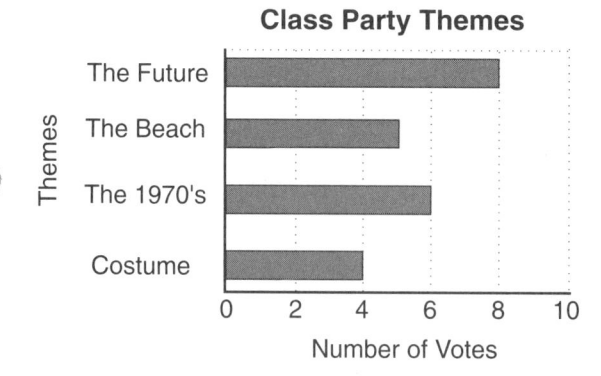

In the bar graph to the left, the longest bar shows that "The Future" received the most votes as Class Party Theme. The shortest bar shows that "Costume" received the least number of votes.

Use the horizontal bar graph shown at the right.

1. Which craft did most students say was their favorite?

   _____

2. How many students chose boot making as their favorite craft demonstration?

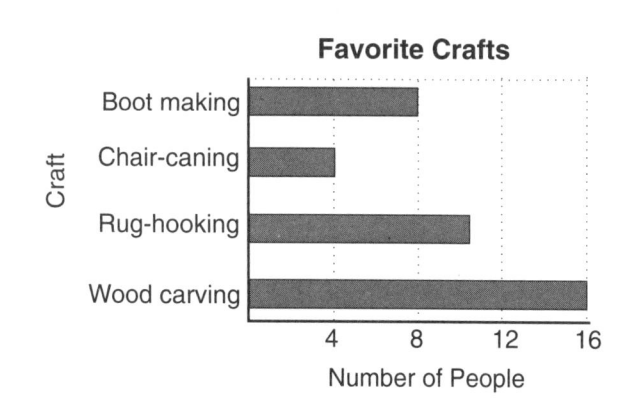

   _____

3. How many more students chose wood carving than chose chair-caning as their favorite crafts? _____

5

Reading and Making a Bar Graph (continued)

4. Make a horizontal bar graph to display the data in the table.

Pizza Toppings Choices

Topping	Votes	Topping	Votes
Pepperoni	30	Onions	20
Mushrooms	40	Olives	4
Sausage	75	Peppers	35

Use the bar graph you made in Question 4.

5. Which topping was chosen the least? _____

6. How many more people chose peppers over pepperoni? _____

7. **Writing in Math** Which bar is twice as long as the bar for onions? What does that mean?

_____

Test Prep Circle the correct letter for the answer.

Mrs. Green divided her class into three reading teams. She created a bar graph to chart the number of books each group read.

8. What is the best label for the bottom of the graph?

   A Number of Books read by Mrs. Green

   B Team

   C Books

   D Number of Books read by the Yellow Team

9. How many more books did the Blue Team read than the Yellow Team?

   A 3   B 6   C 10   D 4

Name _____   Intervention Lesson **L4**

Graphing Ordered Pairs

Example

Use ordered pairs to locate points on a coordinate grid.

How to Name a Point

What ordered pair names where the
Bear Cave is located?
Start at (0, 0).
Move 1 place to the right and
3 places up.
The Bear Cave is located at point (1, 3)
on the grid.

How to Locate a Point

What is located at (3, 2)?
Start at (0, 0)
Move 3 spaces to the right and
2 spaces up.
You are at the Snake Pit.

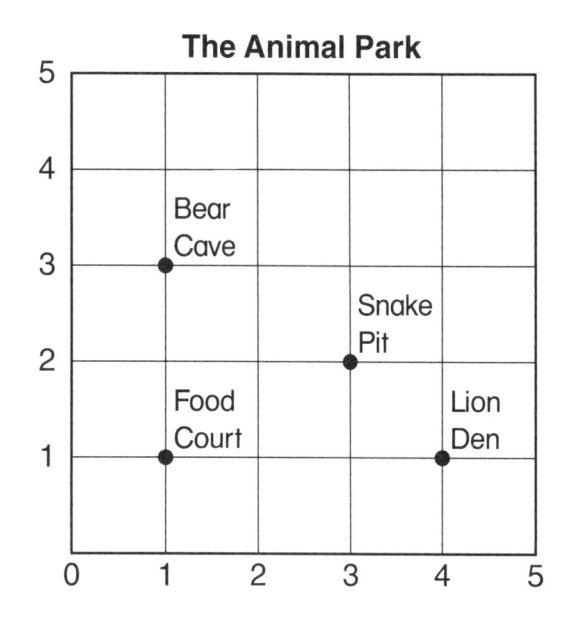

The Animal Park

(grid showing: Bear Cave at (1, 3), Snake Pit at (3, 2), Food Court at (1, 1), Lion Den at (4, 1))

---

1. Write the ordered pair that describes the location of the
   Lion Den. _____

2. What is located at (1, 1)? _____

7

Name _____   Intervention Lesson **L4**

Graphing Ordered Pairs (continued)

Use the grid to answer Questions 3–14.

Write the ordered pair that describes the location of each point.

3. A _____   **4.** B _____

5. C _____   **6.** D _____

7. E _____   **8.** F _____

Write the letter of the point named by each ordered pair.

9. (8, 5) ___   **10.** (4, 9) ___

11. (8, 2) ___   **12.** (5, 7) ___

13. (8, 9) ___   **14.** (7, 6) ___

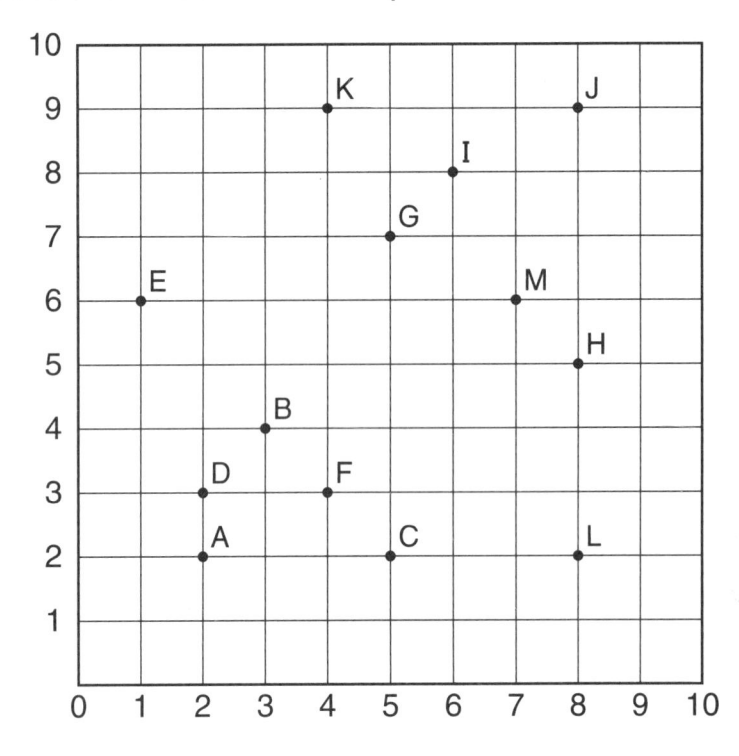

15. Reasoning A grid point is located at (4, 7). If you change the order of these numbers, will the new ordered pair of numbers affect the location on the grid? _____

Test Prep Circle the correct letter for the answer.

Use the grid above to answer Questions 16–17.

16. I is located at this point.

　　A (8, 4)　　**B** (8, 8)　　**C** (6, 8)　　**D** (6, 9)

17. Which letter is located at (8, 2)?

　　A F　　**B** H　　**C** J　　**D** L

8

Name _____

Intervention Lesson **L5**

Reading and Making Line Graphs

Example

Use the line graph at the right:

In what month does Houston have an average rainfall of 4 inches?

June

What is the average rainfall in Houston in September?

5 inches

Between what 2 months does the average rainfall increase the most?

August and September

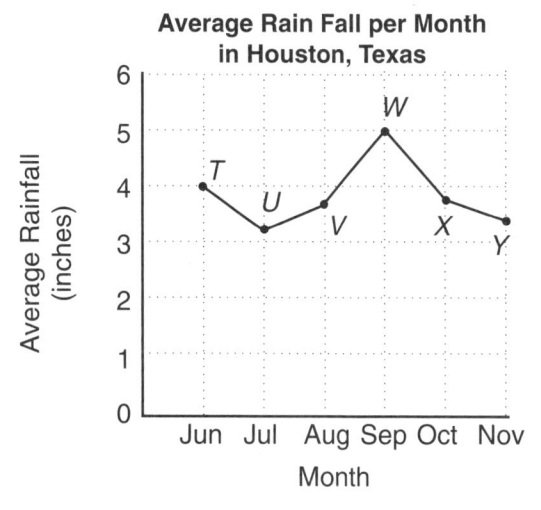

Use the line graph at the right for Questions 1–5.

1. During what month did the Polar Bears win 10 games?

   _____

2. How many games did the Polar Bears win in January?

   _____

3. Between what 2 months did the number of games won increase the most?

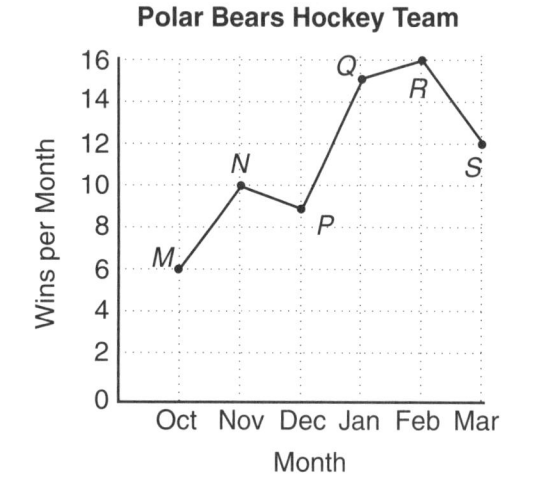

   _____

4. What is the difference between the number of games won in October and the number won in March? _____

5. What does Point *P* represent?

   _____

9

Name _____

Intervention Lesson **L5**

Reading and Making Line Graphs (continued)

Use the graph at the right for Questions 6–8.

Mark's Home Runs

6. In what year did Mark hit 52 home runs?

   _____

7. Between what 2 years did Mark's number of home runs increase the most?

   _____

8. How many home runs did Mark hit in 1998?

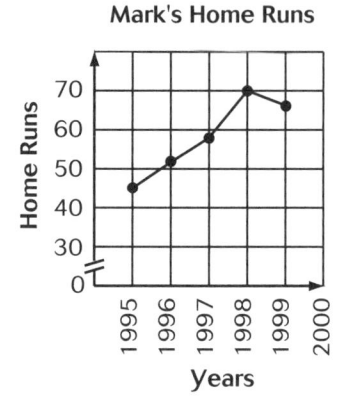

   _____

Use the data in the table at the right for Questions 9 and 10.

9. Make a line graph using this data.

Number of raffle tickets sold

Day	Number
Monday	45
Tuesday	47
Wednesday	52
Thursday	54
Friday	56

10. Between what 2 days was the greatest increase in tickets sold?

    _____

Test Prep Circle the correct letter for the answer.

Use the data and line graph from Exercises 9–10.

11. What trend does the graph show?

    A Ticket sales are decreasing each day.

    B Ticket sales are increasing each day.

    C The cost of tickets is increasing each day.

    D No trends can be determined.

Name _____

Intervention Lesson **L6**

Choosing Appropriate Graphs

Example 1

Different Ways to Display Data

A **bar graph** shows countable data and makes comparisons.
A **line graph** shows changes over time.
A **pictograph** best shows data that is multiples of a number.
A **line plot** compares data by showing clusters of information.
A **circle graph** compares parts of a group to the whole.
A **stem-and-leaf plot** organizes data in numerical order.

What type of graph could you use to display the information given in the table?

A line graph would show the changes over time.

A pictograph would show the data as multiples of 10.

Number of Books Sold	
January	80
February	90
March	70
April	100
May	40

Tell what type of graph would be most appropriate to represent the data and why.

1. Every hour a lifeguard records the number of people in the swimming pool. The pool opens at 1:00 P.M. and closes at 7:00 P.M.

   _____

2. The teacher wants to show what percent of the students own each type of pet.

   _____

11

Name _____

Intervention Lesson **L6**

Choosing Appropriate Graphs (continued)

Tell what type of graph you would choose to represent the data.

3.
Life Expectance of Animals	
Animal	Years
Bull Frog	16
Kangaroo	9
Lion	35
Sheep	15
Tiger	22

_____

4.
Amount Collected for Bake Sale	
Monday	$200
Tuesday	$150
Wednesday	$75
Thursday	$90
Friday	$110

_____

For a math project, Bob constructed a stem-and-leaf plot to show the number of baskets made in two minutes by a group of volunteers shooting basketballs.

Stem	Leaf
0	4 6 8 9
1	0 1 4
2	1

5. Reasoning Is a bar graph a good way to show the data collected? Why or Why not?

_____

_____

Test Prep Circle the correct letter for the answer.

6. Marie has collected the following data. What would be the best way for her to display the data?

    The number of questions answered correctly on a quiz.

    4 5 8 3 4 5 6 9 4 6 9 8 7 3 2 8 7 8

    A circle graph   **C** pictograph

    B line graph   **D** line plot

12

Name _____

Intervention Lesson **L7**

Math Diagnosis and Intervention System

Circle Graphs

Circle graphs show parts of a whole.

Example

Make a circle graph to show the data in the table.

Favorite Type of Book	
Books	Number of Students
Adventure	4
Mystery	5
Biography	2
Poetry	1

Step 1: Draw a circle with 12 equal sectors to represent the total number of students.

Step 2: Color the number of sectors for each type of book a different pattern.

Step 3: Label each section and title the graph.

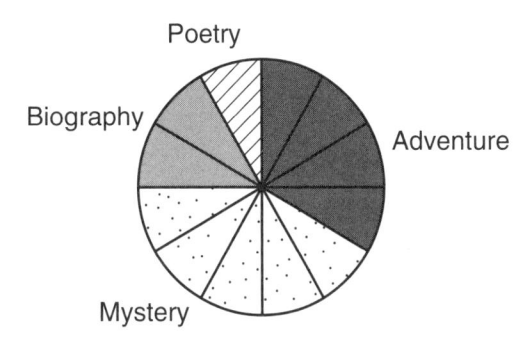

When looking at a graph, think about benchmark fractions.

About $\frac{1}{2}$ of the students chose Mystery books as their favorite; 5 out of 12 is close to 6 out of 12, or $\frac{1}{2}$.

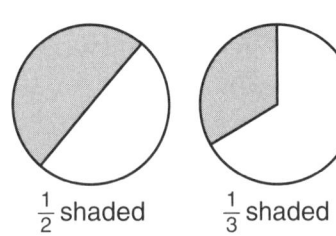

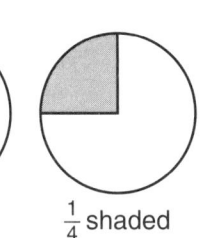

$\frac{1}{2}$ shaded $\frac{1}{3}$ shaded $\frac{1}{4}$ shaded

---

What fraction does the shaded section of graph represent?

1.

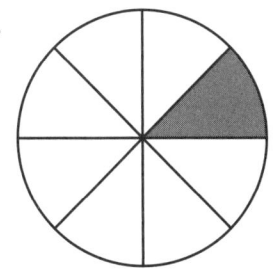

2.

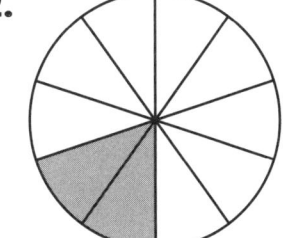

3.

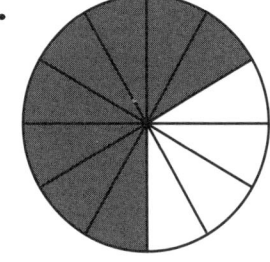

_____   _____   _____

13

Name _____

Intervention Lesson **L7**

Circle Graphs (continued)

Use the graph for Exercises 4–7.

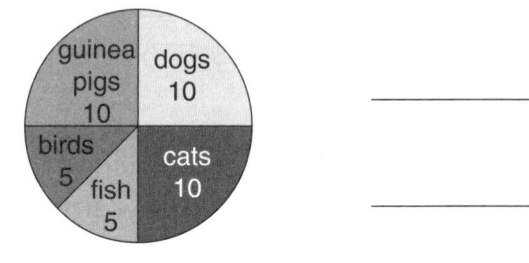

4. How many pets are entered? _____

5. What fraction of the pets entering the pet show are cats? _____

6. What fraction of the pets entered are not dogs or guinea pigs? _____

7. What fraction of pets entered have fur or feathers? _____

Use the graph for Exercises 8 and 9.

Favorite Sports of 10-Year-Old Boys

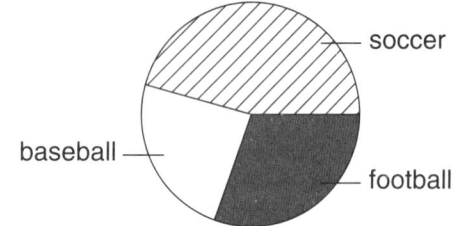

8. If there were 210 boys surveyed, about how many chose football as their favorite sport?

   _____

9. Of the 210 boys surveyed, about how many chose soccer as their favorite? _____

10. **Reasoning** What are two pieces of information you can get from a circle graph?

    _____
    _____
    _____

Test Prep Circle the correct letter for the answer.

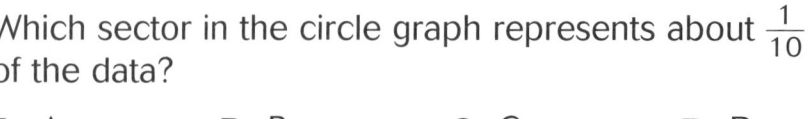

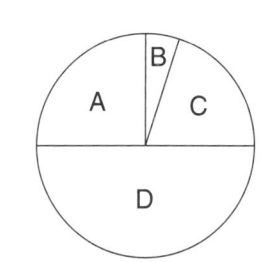

11. Which sector in the circle graph represents about $\frac{1}{10}$ of the data?

    A A   **B** B   **C** C   **D** D

12. What fraction does sector A represent?

    A $\frac{3}{4}$ **B** $\frac{1}{2}$ **C** $\frac{1}{4}$ **D** $\frac{1}{10}$

14

Name _____   Intervention Lesson **L8**

Double Bar Graphs

Example

Use the graph at the right to answer the questions.

What trend does the graph show?
The number of both types of stations is increasing.

Between which two consecutive years did the number of News/Talk Stations surpass the number of Rock Stations?
Between 1991 and 1992

Between which two consecutive years did the greatest increase in the number of rock stations occur?
Between 1990 and 1991

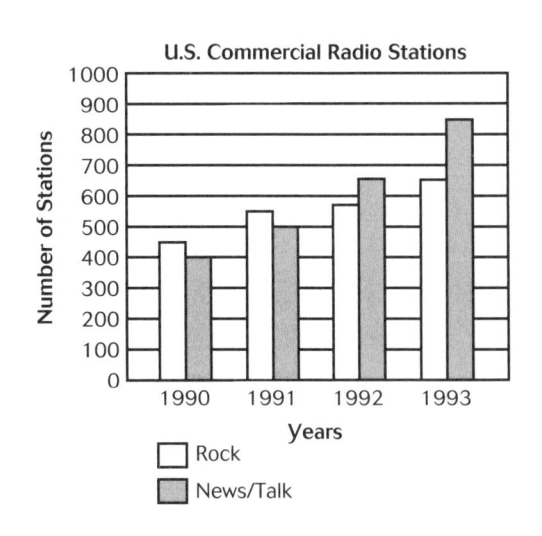

Use the graph at the right to answer Questions 1–4.

1. What does each pair of bars represent?

   _____

   _____

2. For which item were the most boxes sold?

   _____

3. How many more caramels did 5th graders sell as compared to 6th graders?

   _____

4. Which type of box had the most sales for 5th graders? _____

   Which type of box had the most sales for 6th graders? _____

15

Double Bar Graphs (continued)

Use the graph at the right to answer Questions 5–9.

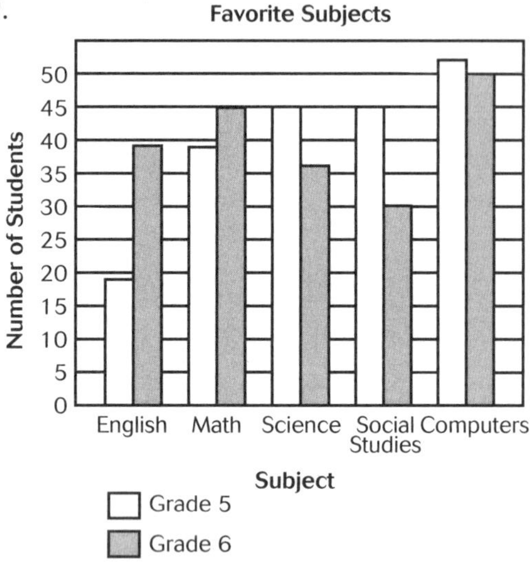

5. What does each pair of bars represent.

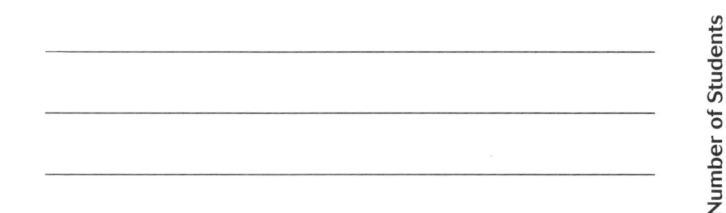

   _____

   _____

   _____

6. For which subject is the difference in choice the greatest?

   _____

Favorite Subjects

Number of Students vs Subject (English, Math, Science, Social Studies, Computers)
☐ Grade 5
■ Grade 6

7. Which subject was chosen as favorite the most?

   _____

8. What subject was least popular with 5th graders? _____

   What subject was least popular with 6th graders? _____

9. **Mental Math** What was the total number of students who chose Math as their favorite subject? _____

Test Prep Circle the correct letter for the answer.

The data in this table will be used to make a double bar graph.

State Fair Attendance

Day	1996	1997
Friday	8,500	10,000
Saturday	10,000	14,000
Sunday	12,000	14,000
Monday	7,000	9,000
Tuesday	3,500	8,000
Wednesday	4,000	8,500
Thursday	4,500	9,000

10. In the graph, the attendance figures will be shown on the vertical scale. What information should be shown on the horizontal scale?

    A Years   **C** Days of the week

    B Weeks   **D** Admission price

11. Which scale would be best for the attendance figure on the vertical axis?

    A 10   **C** 500

    B 100   **D** 2,000

Name _____

Intervention Lesson **L9**

Scatterplots

Example

Chihuahua Puppy Weight	
Age	Weight (ounces)
Birth (0)	5
4 weeks	19
8 weeks	29
12 weeks	41
16 weeks	54

The table at the right shows the ages of a Chihuahua puppy and its weight as it grows.

Is there a pattern or trend? One way to see a pattern is to plot the data as ordered pairs.

Step 1: Write a title and label the axes.

Step 2: Mark the intervals on the *x*-axis and *y*-axis.

Step 3: Plot each point.

What type of pattern can be seen? As the age of the puppy increases along the *x*-axis, its weight is also increasing along the *y*-axis.

There are three types of patterns in scatterplots.

Positive Pattern 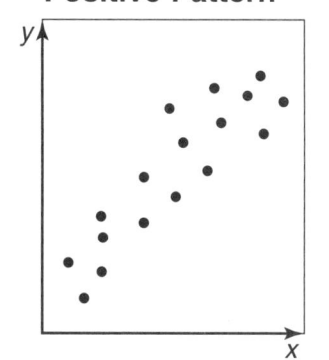
Both values increase

Negative Pattern 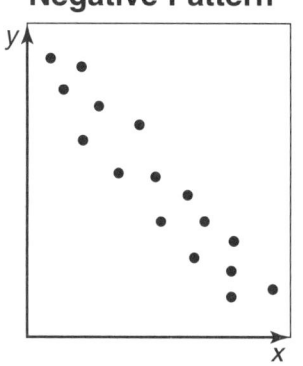
One value increases, the other decreases

No Pattern or Trend 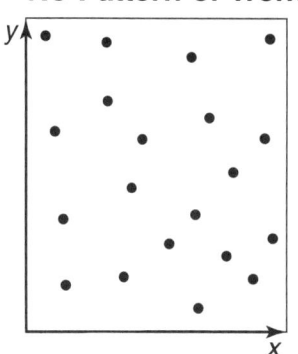
No general trend

1. This table shows the hours studied and scores received on a test. Make a scatterplot. What is the pattern? What is the trend?

Hours Studied	0.5	1	1.5	2	0.5	2	1.5	1
Test Score	12	16	19	20	8	19	16	15

_____

_____

17

Intervention Lesson **L9**

Scatterplots (continued)

2. The table below shows the time and the outside temperature. Make a scatterplot of the data. Do the points lie in a rough pattern? If so, what trend is suggested by the scatterplot?

Time	Temperature (°F)
5 P.M.	20
6 P.M.	18
7 P.M.	13
8 P.M.	12
9 P.M.	10

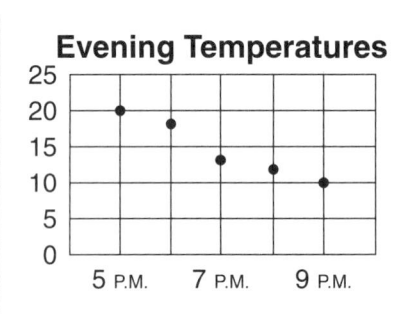

_____
_____

Tell what trends you might see in scatterplots of the following data.

3. The number of hours children sleep and the length of their school days.

4. The size of a candle and the time after it was lit.

Test Prep Circle the correct letter for the answer.

5. Which new point most likely will be a point on the scatterplot?

A (8, 100)

B (1, 370)

C (1000, 4)

D (9, 900)

6. What type of trend is shown in the scatterplot?

A positive **B** negative **C** no trend

Name _____   Intervention Lesson **L10**

Understanding Probability

Example 1

Is picking a tile with an X out of Bag A certain or impossible?

There are only tiles with O's in Bag A, so it is impossible to pick a tile with an X.

A

Example 2

Is picking a tile with an X out of Bag B more likely or less likely?

There are 5 tiles with Xs and only 1 with an O, so it is more likely that an X tile will be chosen.

B

Write whether picking a tile with an X is certain, impossible, more likely, or less likely.

1.

2.

3.

_____   _____   _____

4.

5.

6.

_____   _____   _____

19

Name _____

Intervention Lesson **L10**

Understanding Probability (continued)

Suppose you drop a cube numbered 1–6. Tell whether the following are certain, impossible, more likely, or less likely.

7. The cube will land showing a 2.   _____

8. The cube will land showing a 9.   _____

9. The cube will land showing a 1.   _____

10. The cube will land showing a number less than 5.   _____

Write whether each is impossible or certain.

11. A student who is 8 will be 9 years old in a year.   _____

12. A coin tossed in the air lands on neither heads nor tails.   _____

13. A pig will fly on its own.   _____

Write whether each is more likely or less likely.

14. You will take a drink of water today.   _____

15. You will ride on a horse tomorrow.   _____

Test Prep Circle the correct letter for the answer.

16. Which of the following events is most likely?

　A Monday will come after Tuesday.

　B You will win a TV today.

　C You will eat some food today.

　D You will drive a car tomorrow.

Name _____

Intervention Lesson **L11**

Fair and Unfair

Example 1

Give the chance that the spinner will land on B.

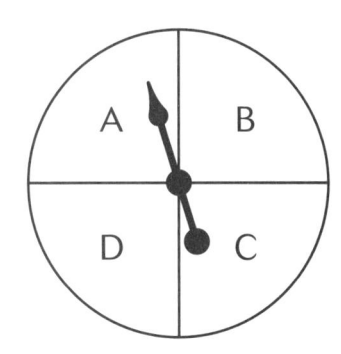

There are 4 equal sections in all.

One section has the letter B.

So, there is a 1 out of 4 chance that the spinner will land on the letter B.

Example 2

Give the chance of each outcome for the spinner.

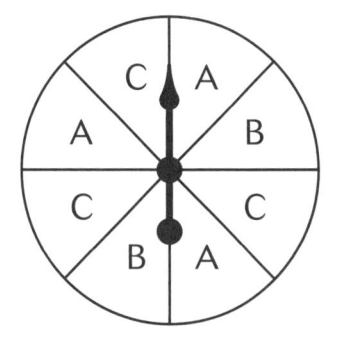

There are 8 equal sections in all.

There is a 3 out of 8 chance that the spinner will land on A.

There is a 2 out of 8 chance that the spinner will land on B.

There is a 3 out of 8 chance that the spinner will land on C.

Use the spinner for Questions 1–3. Give the chance of each outcome.

1. The letter D ____ out of ____

2. The letter E ____ out of ____

3. The letter F ____ out of ____

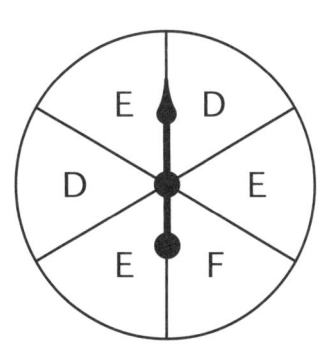

21

Name _____

Intervention Lesson **L11**

Fair and Unfair (continued)

Use Spinner A for Questions 4–6.

Give the chance that the spinner will land on each outcome.

4. J
___ out of ___

5. L
___ out of ___

6. K
___ out of ___

Spinner A

7. Writing in Math Two players take turns spinning spinner B. Player 1 scores a point if the spinner lands on an even number. Player 2 scores a point if the spinner lands on an odd number. Is this game fair for this spinner? Explain why or why not.

_____
_____

Spinner B

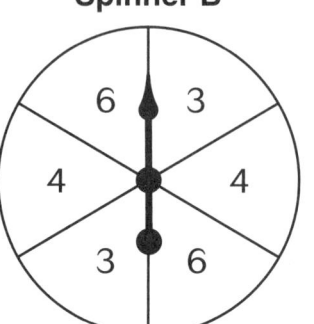

Test Prep Circle the correct letter for the answer.

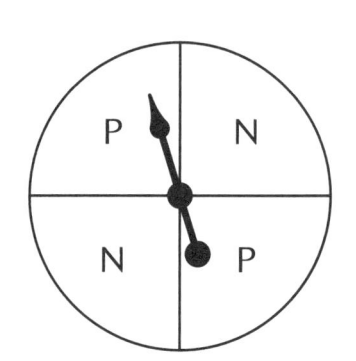

8. Give the chance that the spinner will land on N.

   A 1 out of 3   **B** 2 out of 2
   C 2 out of 4   **D** 1 out of 4

9. Give the chance that the spinner will land on P.

   A 2 out of 3   **B** 2 out of 2
   C 1 out of 4   **D** 2 out of 4

Name _____

Intervention Lesson **L12**

Math Diagnosis and Intervention System

Finding Probability

Example

Look at the spinner.

What is the probability of spinning an even number?

There are 10 possible outcomes: 1, 2, 3, 4, 5, 6, 7, 8, 9, 10.

There are 5 outcomes that are even numbers: 2, 4, 6, 8, 10.

$\frac{5}{10}$ $\frac{\text{number of ways to spin an even number}}{\text{total number of outcomes}}$

The probability of spinning an even number is $\frac{5}{10}$ or $\frac{1}{2}$.

Refer to the spinner above. Write the probability of spinning:

1. 3

2. 0

3. an odd number

4. a number greater than 4

5. a prime number

6. 12

7. a number less than 11

8. a multiple of 3

23

Name _____

Intervention Lesson **L12**

Math Diagnosis and Intervention System

Finding Probability (continued)

Refer to the bag at the right. Write the probability of choosing:

(bag containing letters: M, A, T, H, E, M, A, T, I, C, S)

9. an M

10. a vowel

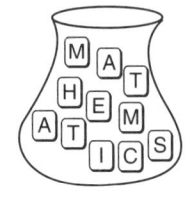

_____ _____

11. an M, A, T, or H

12. an N

_____ _____

13. Suppose a bag contains 4 red tiles, 5 yellow tiles, and 1 blue tile. What is the chance of picking each color?

_____

14. Suppose a jar contains 5 white marbles, 4 black marbles, and 3 red marbles. What is the chance of picking each color?

_____

15. Reasoning Draw a spinner in which the probability of spinning an X is 1 out of 4, and spinning a Y is 2 out of 4.

16. You are one of 35 people in a drawing. What is the chance that you will be chosen? _____

Test Prep Circle the correct letter for the answer.

17. Suppose a bag contains 3 blue tiles, 4 red tiles, and 3 white tiles. What are the chances of choosing a blue tile?

A $\frac{3}{10}$ **B** $\frac{4}{10}$ **C** $\frac{4}{7}$ **D** $\frac{3}{7}$

24

Name _____

Intervention Lesson **L13**

Understanding Probability

Example 1

How likely is it to pull a tile showing an odd number out of the bag?

There are only even numbers on the tiles in the bag, so it is **impossible** to pull an odd-numbered tile.

Example 2

How likely is it to pull a tile showing an odd number out of the bag?

There are 8 tiles with odd numbers and only 2 tiles with even numbers, so it is **more likely** to pull an odd-numbered tile.

For each bag, use the words impossible, less likely, equally likely, more likely, or certain to describe how likely it is to pull a triangle from the bag.

1. 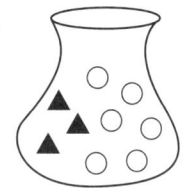
2. 
3.

4. 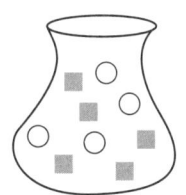
5. 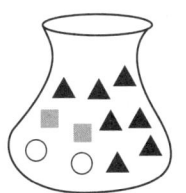
6.

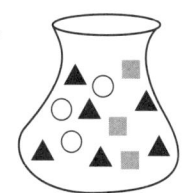

25

Name _____ Intervention Lesson **L13**

Understanding Probability (continued)

You have 8 cards in a box. Three cards are blue, 2 cards are yellow, 2 cards are green, and 1 card is orange. Tell whether the following are impossible, less likely, equally likely, more likely, or certain.

7. You pick a colored card. _____

8. You pick an orange or a blue card. _____

9. You pick a green card. _____

10. You pick a purple card. _____

Suppose you spin the spinner shown at the right. Tell whether the following are impossible, less likely, equally likely, more likely, or certain.

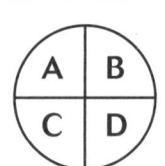

11. Spinning A, B, or C. _____

12. Spinning D. _____

13. Spinning a number. _____

14. Spinning a letter. _____

15. Math Reasoning Draw a spinner for which the chance of spinning A, B, or C is equally likely.

Test Prep Circle the correct letter for the answer.

16. Which of the following events is impossible?

   A A seed will grow into a plant.

   B A butterfly will become a bird.

   C A chicken will hatch from an egg.

   D A dog will bark.

Name _____

Intervention Lesson **L14**

Listing Outcomes

Example 1

Look at Spinner 1.

Name all the possible outcomes of a spin.

The spinner could land on stripes, dots, or crosses.

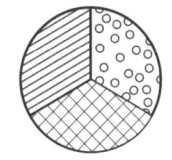

Example 2

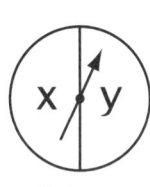

Look at Spinner 2.

Name all the possible outcomes of spinning Spinner 1 and then 2.

You can make a tree diagram or a table to show all the possible outcomes.

```
Spinner 1    Spinner 2    Possible Outcomes
stripes  ───── X           stripes, X
         ╲     y           stripes, y
dots     ───── X           dots, X
         ╲     y           dots, y
crosses  ───── X           crosses, X
         ╲     y           crosses, y
```

	X	y
stripes	stripes, X	stripes, y
dots	dots, X	dots, y
crosses	crosses, X	crosses, y

List all possible outcomes for each situation.

1.  (Spinner with 4, 1, 1, 2, 3, 5, 2, 6)

2.  (Spinner with L, M, N)

3. (Vase with letters X, Y, A, B, Z, X, A, Z, C, B)

_____

_____

27

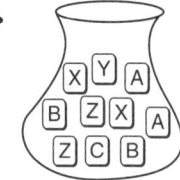

Name _____

Math Diagnosis and Intervention System

Intervention Lesson **L14**

Listing Outcomes (continued)

List all possible outcomes for each situation.

4.

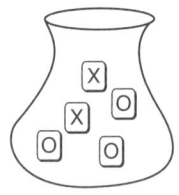

5.

6.

_____   _____   _____

_____   _____   _____

_____   _____   _____

7. Rosie chooses a tile from the bag in Exercise 4 and then chooses a marble from the bag in #5. Make a tree diagram or a table to show all possible outcomes.

8. Jason chooses a tile from the bag in #4 and then spins the spinner in #6. Make a tree diagram or a table to show all possible outcomes.

9. **Math Reasoning** When performing 2 tasks as in Exercises 7 and 8, what is the relationship between the number of outcomes of the 2 tasks and the number of outcomes of the 2 tasks together? _____

_____

Test Prep Circle the correct letter for the answer.

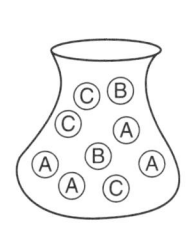

10. Andy flips a coin and then draws a marble from the bag at the right. What are the possible outcomes?

   A Heads, A; Tails, B; Heads, C

   B Heads, A; Heads, B; Heads, C; Tails, A; Tails, B; Tails, C

   C Heads; Tails; A; B; C

   D Heads, A; Heads, B; Heads, C; Tails, C

28

Name _____

Intervention Lesson **L15**

Math Diagnosis and Intervention System

Displaying Probability Data and Making Predictions

Example

Use the bar graph at the right to answer the questions.

What does each bar on the graph show?
   Each bar shows the number of each type of pet.

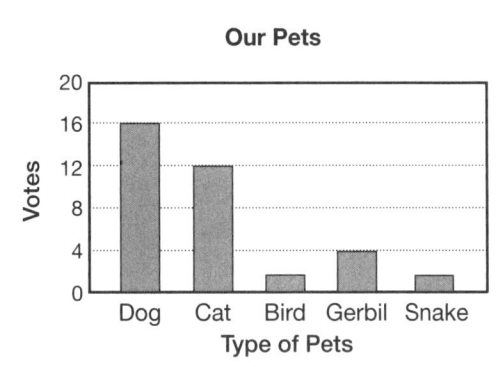

What pet is most common among these students?
   Dog is the highest bar, so it is the most common.

What pet is the least common?
   Bird and Snake are both the same height and are both the lowest bar, so must be the least common.

If you repeated the voting, what answer do you think would be the most common?
   Dog.

Use the bar graph at the right for Questions 1–4.

1. What does each bar on the graph show?

   _____

2. What type of fish was caught most often? _____

3. What type of fish was caught least often? _____

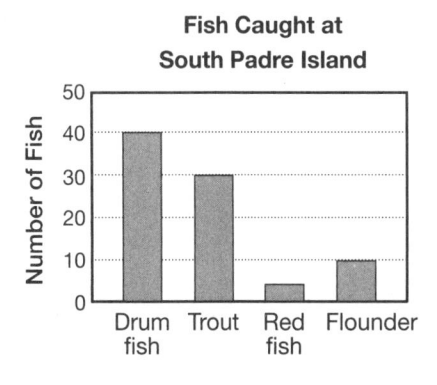

4. If you went to South Padre Island and watched the boats come in, what kind of fish would you be most likely to see?

   _____

29

Name _____

Intervention Lesson **L15**

Displaying Probability Data and Making Predictions (continued)

Use the line plot at the right for Questions 5–9.

```
                        X
                        X
              X         X         X
            X X         X         X                  X
          +---+---+---+---+---+---+---+---+---+
          0   2   4   6   8  10  12  14  16
```

5. What is the most common number of points scored by players on this basketball team?

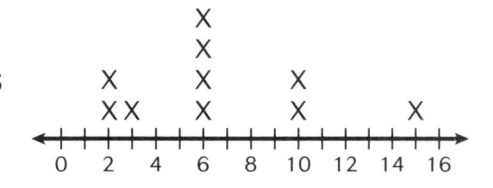

_____

6. What is the least common number of points scored by players on this basketball team? _____

7. Does the data in the line plot form any clusters? Explain.

_____

8. How many players are represented by this line plot? _____

9. Math Reasoning Predict how many players out of 20 would score 10 points per game. _____

10. Use the following data to make a bar graph.

Favorite National Parks

National Parks	Tally
Davy Crockett	IIII
Yellowstone	ĦĦ ĦĦ II
Grand Canyon	ĦĦ IIII
Sam Houston	ĦĦ I

Test Prep Circle the correct letter for the answer.

11. What does the length of the bars represent on the bar graph in Exercise 10?

    A Number of National Forests   **C** Number of votes

    B Number of students   **D** Number of members

Name _____

Intervention Lesson **L16**

Math Diagnosis and Intervention System

Predictions and Probability

A number cube has sides labeled 2, 3, 4, 5, 6, and 7.

Example 1

Compare the chances of tossing an odd number to a number less than 4.

Event: tossing an odd number

Favorable Outcomes: 3, 5, 7

3 out of 6 possible outcomes are favorable, so in 3 out of 6 tosses, you can expect an odd number.

Event: tossing a number less than 4

Favorable Outcomes: 2, 3

2 out of 6 possible outcomes are favorable, so in 2 out of 6 tosses, you can expect a 2 or 3.

Tossing a number less than 4 is **less likely** than tossing an odd number.
Tossing an odd number is **more likely** than tossing a number less than 4.

Example 2

In 100 tosses, how many times would you expect an odd number?
How many odd outcomes are there? 3 out of 6

3 out of 6 is the same as 1 out of 2, so in 100 tosses we would expect about 50 tosses to be an odd number.

Use the spinner for Questions 1–4.

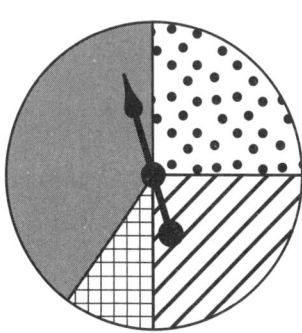

1. What are the possible outcomes?

   _____

2. Are the outcomes equally likely? Why or why not?

   _____

3. What color would you expect to occur most often? Least often?

   _____

4. In 100 spins, how many times would you expect stripes?

   _____

31

Intervention Lesson **L16**

Name _____

Predictions and Probability (continued)

Use the spinner for Questions 5–9. Tell whether each event is equally likely, likely, unlikely, certain, or impossible.

5. dotted or striped

   _____

6. checked

   _____

7. red

   _____

8. gray or dotted

   _____

9. gray, striped, dotted, or checked

   _____

Use the given information for Questions 10–11.

Mr. Ohme has a jar of marbles sitting on his desk. There are 15 red marbles, 3 blue marbles, 6 green marbles, and 1 purple marble.

10. If you were to close your eyes and draw a marble, what are the possible outcomes?

    _____

11. If you drew a marble from the jar, is each outcome equally likely?

    _____

Test Prep Circle the correct letter for the answer.

12. Mrs. Thompson baked some cookies. She has 4 dozen chocolate chip, 3 dozen sugar, and 1 dozen oatmeal. Describe the chance of her giving her daughter an oatmeal cookie.

    A Certain   **B** Impossible   **C** Unlikely   **D** Likely

32

Predicting Outcomes

Example

There are blue, white, and striped socks in a drawer. There are 10 socks in all. Socks were removed from the drawer, then replaced. The results of the experiment are shown in the table.

Blue								
White	|||| |||| |||| |||| |||| |||| |||| |||| |||| |||| ||||	
Striped							

What is the probability that the next sock chosen will be blue? There were 76 socks drawn and 8 of them were blue. The probability that the next one chosen will be blue is $\frac{8}{76}$ or $\frac{2}{19}$.

There are 54 beads of 3 colors: orange, purple, and pink. Beads are drawn from the bag and replaced. Use the chart at the right to find the probability of each choice.

Orange											
Purple													
Pink	|||| |||| |||| |||| |||| ||

1. orange

2. purple

3. pink

4. not orange

5. purple or pink

6. not pink

7. not green

8. blue

9. not purple

10. orange or pink

11. orange or purple

12. orange, pink, or purple

Name _____

Intervention Lesson **L17**

Predicting Outcomes (continued)

Maureen counted the colors of cars that were in the school's parking lot. Here is the data she recorded. Find the probability that the next car will be each color.

Car Colors

red	|||| |||| ||
blue	|||| |||| |||| ||
black	|||| ||
green	|||| ||||
gold	||||

13. red

14. green or gold

_____   _____

15. blue

16. not black

_____   _____

17. green, black, or blue

18. not red or blue

_____   _____

19. Veronica conducted a survey in which she asked 35 people to choose their favorite food category. 10 chose Mexican, 15 chose Italian, and 10 chose Chinese. Based on this survey, what is the probability that the next person surveyed will choose Mexican as their favorite food category? _____

20. Math Reasoning When asked their favorite subject, half selected Computers. What is the probability that a student's favorite subject will not be Computers? _____

Test Prep Circle the correct letter for the answer.

21. There are 10 beads of 4 colors in a bag. Beads are drawn from the bag and replaced. These are the results: gray—4, brown—12, black—12, yellow—32. What is the probability that the next choice will be brown?

A $\frac{1}{5}$ **B** $\frac{4}{10}$ **C** $\frac{12}{10}$ **D** $\frac{1}{4}$

Name _____

Intervention Lesson **L18**

Finding Probability

Example

Look at the spinner.

What is the probability of spinning a triangle?

There are 8 possible outcomes:
square, triangle, circle, star, circle, triangle, triangle, star.

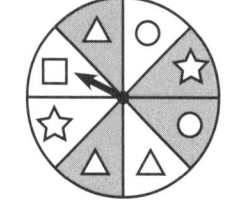

There are 3 outcomes that are triangles.

Probability of spinning a triangle = $\dfrac{\text{number of favorable outcomes}}{\text{number of possible outcomes}} = \dfrac{3}{8}$

The probability of spinning a triangle is $\dfrac{3}{8}$.

Refer to the spinner above. What is the probability that the pointer will stop on each of the following?

1. circle

2. star

3. square

4. shaded section

5. circle or triangle

6. octagon

7. shaded section with star

8. a shape

35

Name _____

Intervention Lesson **L18**

Finding Probability (continued)

Refer to the bag at the right. What is the probability of choosing each of the following?

9. an M
10. a consonant

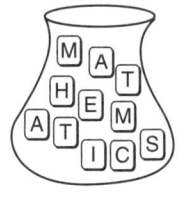

_____   _____

11. an S, E, or T
12. not an N

_____   _____

13. Suppose a bag contains 2 red tiles, 5 yellow tiles, and 1 blue tile. What is the chance of picking each color?

_____

14. Suppose a jar contains 3 striped socks, 8 solid socks, and 2 dotted socks. What is the chance of picking each type?

_____

15. **Math Reasoning** Draw a spinner in which the probability of spinning black is 1 out of 6, and spinning a gray is 3 out of 6.

16. There are 120 people at a gathering. What is the probability that you will be chosen for one of the 5 door prizes? _____

Test Prep Circle the correct letter for the answer.

17. Suppose a bag contains 5 blue marbles, 4 red marbles, and 3 white marbles. What are the chances of choosing a red marble?

   A $\frac{4}{8}$ **B** $\frac{4}{10}$ **C** $\frac{1}{3}$ **D** $\frac{3}{12}$

36

Name _____

Intervention Lesson **L19**

Counting Methods

Example

A fruit snack can be made with one choice of fruit and one choice of yogurt. There are 4 different kinds of fresh fruits: strawberries, banana slices, pineapple chunks, and orange slices. The flavors of yogurt are lemon or vanilla.

How many different fruit snacks are possible?

You can draw a tree diagram to represent the different kinds of snacks.

strawberries — lemon
              — vanilla
banana — lemon
       — vanilla
pineapple — lemon
          — vanilla
orange — lemon
       — vanilla

You can represent the snacks in a grid.

	lemon	vanilla
strawberries	straw., lemon	straw., vanilla
banana	banana, lemon	banana, vanilla
pineapple	pineap., lemon	pineap., vanilla
orange	orange, lemon	orange, vanilla

A third way is to use the counting principle. There are 4 outcomes for the first event and 2 outcomes for the second event, so there are 4×2 total possible outcomes.

There are 8 possible outcomes.

Assume you randomly choose one of the options above. Find each probability as a fraction and as a percent to the nearest whole percent.

1. *P*(banana, lemon)

2. *P*(banana vanilla or orange lemon)

3. *P*(lemon)

37

Intervention Lesson **L19**

Counting Methods (continued)

4. A store sells long-sleeved and short-sleeved T-shirts. The T-shirts come in the colors white, black, yellow, and gray. Draw a tree diagram or table to show the possible combinations of shirts. How many possible combinations are there? _____

Assume you randomly choose one of the options in Exercise 4. Find each probability as a fraction and as a percent to the nearest whole percent.

5. *P*(long-sleeved black shirt)

6. *P*(short-sleeved white or gray shirt)

_____   _____

Use the table to answer Exercises 7–9.

7. **Mental Math** Find the number of possible outcomes for a juice and eggs.

Juices	Eggs	Breads
orange grapefruit apple	scrambled hard-boiled	bran muffin whole wheat toast bagel

_____

8. Find the number of possible outcomes for a juice, eggs, and breads. _____

9. Find the probability you get apple juice with a bagel when you randomly select a juice, eggs, and bread. _____

Test Prep Circle the correct letter for the answer.

10. Find the number of possible outcomes for selecting a juice and bread from the table above.

    A 6   **B** 9   **C** 18   **D** 8

Name _____

Intervention Lesson **L20**

Permutations and Combinations

Example

Decide whether or not order matters in the following situation.
Choosing 3 club members to serve on a committee.

Because the committee members do not have any titles or special roles, order does not matter.

Decide whether or not order matters in each situation.

1. Choosing 2 books to read from a shelf of 15 books

_____

2. Choosing a president, vice-president, and secretary from 12 club members

_____

3. Choosing 3 elective classes to take from a list of 10 classes

_____

4. Choosing an arrangement of 5 toys on a shelf from a box of 30 toys

_____

5. Choosing an arrangement of 4 flowers from 7 different varieties

_____

6. Choosing a line up of 10 band members to march in the front row from 25 band members

_____

7. Choosing 3 room monitors from 18 students in the class

_____

Name _____

Intervention Lesson **L20**

Permutations and Combinations (continued)

Decide whether or not order matters in each situation.

8. Choosing 9 players to play the different positions in the baseball field from 12 players

_____

9. Choosing 4 students to fill out a survey from a room of 25 students

_____

10. Choosing 10 people to call from a list of 50 people

_____

11. Choosing and scheduling 5 people to interview from 50 applicants

_____

12. Choosing an arrangement of 5 books on a shelf from a box of 30 books

_____

13. Brian is trying to make 3-letter combinations from the letters in the word HORSE. How many permutations are possible? _____

14. Carla has 5 close friends but she can only invite 2 of them on a special outing. How many choices are possible? _____

Test Prep Circle the correct letter for the answer.

15. Find the situation in which order does not matter.

    A Choosing 5 people to be class officers

    B Choosing 3 numbers for a combination lock

    C Choosing 4 people to serve on a committee

    D Choosing 9 players for a batting lineup

Name _____

Intervention Lesson **L21**

Representing Probability

Example

There are red, yellow, blue, and orange cubes in a bag. Lenore pulled one cube at a time from the bag without looking, recorded the result, and then replaced it. She did this 20 times. The results are shown in the table.

Color	Red	Yellow	Blue	Orange
Tally	IIII	IIII III	II	IIII I

Find *P*(blue) as a fraction, a decimal, and a percent.

$P(\text{blue}) = \frac{2}{20}$ $\frac{\text{number of favorable outcomes}}{\text{number of possible outcomes}}$

$= \frac{1}{10}$

To write $\frac{1}{10}$ as a decimal, divide 1 by 10.

$1 \div 10 = 0.1$

To write $\frac{1}{10}$ as a percent, move the decimal point two places to the right and add the % sign.

$\frac{1}{10} = 0.1 = 10\%$

Lenore chooses one cube from the bag described above. Find each probability as a fraction, a decimal, and a percent.

1. *P*(red)

2. *P*(blue or yellow)

_____   _____

3. *P*(not orange)

4. *P*(not red)

_____   _____

5. *P*(yellow)

6. *P*(red or blue)

_____   _____

Representing Probability (continued)

A marble is chosen from the jars without looking. Find each probability as a fraction, a decimal, and a percent.

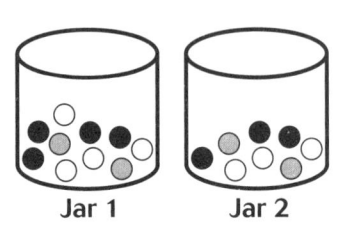

7. *P*(black from Jar 1)   8. *P*(black from Jar 2)

_____   _____

9. *P*(gray from Jar 1)   10. *P*(not gray from Jar 2)

_____   _____

11. *P*(not white from Jar 1)   12. *P*(gray or white from Jar 1)

_____   _____

13. Are you more likely to get a black marble from Jar 1 or Jar 2? Explain.

_____

_____

_____

14. **Math Reasoning** If you have a spinner with red, white, and blue, does adding a black section increase or decrease the probability of spinning red, white, or blue? Explain.

_____

Test Prep Circle the correct letter for the answer.

15. Find the probability of choosing a white marble from Jar 2 above.

     A 62.5%   **B** 40%   **C** 37.5%   **D** 12.5%

Name _____

Intervention Lesson **L22**

Adding Probabilities

Example

You choose 2 cards at random from a set of 8 cards numbered 1–8. Tell whether the events are mutually exclusive. Then, find the probability as a fraction and a percent.

P(5 or even number)

These 2 events cannot happen at the same time so they are mutually exclusive. We can add their probabilities.

$P(5) = \frac{1}{8}$ $P(\text{even number}) = \frac{4}{8}$

$P(5 \text{ or even number}) = P(5) + P(\text{even number}) = \frac{1}{8} + \frac{4}{8} = \frac{5}{8}$

$5 \div 8 = 0.625 = 62.5\%$

So, the probability of these mutually exclusive events is $\frac{5}{8}$ or 62.5%.

You choose 2 cards at random from a set of 10 cards numbered 1–10. Tell whether the events are mutually exclusive. Then, find the probability as a fraction and a percent.

1. $P(1 \text{ or } 3)$

_____

2. $P(5 \text{ or } 6)$

_____

3. $P(\text{an odd number or } 7)$

_____

43

Name _____ Intervention Lesson **L22**

Adding Probabilities (continued)

You toss a number cube twice labeled with the numbers 1–6. Tell whether the events are mutually exclusive. Then, find the probability as a fraction and a percent.

4. $P(3 \text{ or } 4)$

_____

5. $P(1 \text{ or number less than } 3)$

_____

6. $P(\text{even or } 3)$

_____

7. $P(\text{number less than } 3 \text{ or number greater than } 3)$

_____

8. Math Reasoning The probability that it will rain today is 25%. The probability that it will rain tomorrow is 75%. Mark concludes that the probability it will rain in the next 2 days is 100%. Is he right? Why or why not?

_____

_____

Test Prep Circle the correct letter for the answer.

9. You choose a cube from a bag of 8 cubes labeled with letters A–H. Which of the following are mutually exclusive?

   A Choosing a vowel or A   **C** Choosing a consonant or H

   B Choosing A or E   **D** Choosing a vowel or E

10. The probability of 2 mutually exclusive events is $\frac{2}{5}$ and $\frac{1}{5}$. What is the probability that neither of these events will happen?

   A $\frac{3}{5}$ **B** $\frac{1}{5}$ **C** $\frac{2}{5}$ **D** $\frac{5}{5}$

Name _____

Intervention Lesson **L23**

Independent Events

Example

In a game of chance, players spin the spinner at the right twice and record their results.

Find the probability of spinning 5 both times.

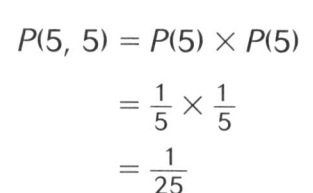

$P(5, 5) = P(5) \times P(5)$

$= \dfrac{1}{5} \times \dfrac{1}{5}$

$= \dfrac{1}{25}$

Find the probability of the following using the spinner above.

1. $P(2, 3)$ **2.** $P(1, \text{not } 1)$ **3.** $P(3, 3)$

4. $P(1, 6)$ **5.** $P(\text{not } 5, \text{not } 5)$ **6.** $P(\text{not } 3, 3)$

7. $P(\text{not } 1, \text{not } 5)$ **8.** $P(0, 1)$ **9.** $P(1 \text{ or } 2, \text{not } 3)$

Name _____

Intervention Lesson **L23**

Math Diagnosis and Intervention System

Independent Events (continued)

Players pick a letter from the bag without looking. They record it and put it back. Then they pick another letter in the same way. Find the probability of the following.

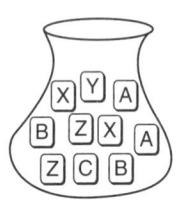

10. $P(A, A)$ **11.** $P(X, y)$ **12.** $P(A, \text{not } X)$

13. $P(\text{not } A, \text{not } A)$ **14.** $P(C, y)$ **15.** $P(\text{not } C, \text{not } y)$

16. In a game of chance, you must toss a 6 on a number cube two times in order to win. The probability of not tossing a 6 is $\frac{5}{6}$. What is the probability of winning? _____

17. Math Reasoning If the probability of spinning red twice on a spinner is $\frac{9}{25}$, then what is the probability of spinning red just once? _____

Test Prep Circle the correct letter for the answer.

18. The probability of choosing a 7 from a bag of cards is $\frac{1}{10}$. What is the probability of choosing a 7 and then not choosing a 7?

     A $\frac{1}{9}$ **B** $\frac{9}{100}$ **C** $\frac{7}{10}$ **D** 1

Intervention Lesson **L24**

Dependent Events

Example

These game cards on the right are put in a bag. You select one without looking, replace it, and select another one. Find the probability of selecting 5, then 5 again.

| 1 | 3 | 2 | 2 |
| 4 | 4 | 5 | 5 |

$P(5, 5) = \dfrac{2}{8} \times \dfrac{2}{8} = \dfrac{4}{64} = \dfrac{1}{16}$

Now find the probability if the game card isn't replaced.

$P(5, 5) = \dfrac{2}{8} \times \dfrac{1}{7} = \dfrac{2}{56} = \dfrac{1}{28}$

The game cards above are put in a bag. You select one without looking, replace it, and select another one. Find the probability of the following.

1. $P(2, 3)$ **2.** $P(1, \text{not } 1)$ **3.** $P(3, 3)$

_____ _____ _____

The game cards above are put in a bag. You select one without looking, do *not* replace it, and select another one. Find the probability of the following.

4. $P(2, 3)$ **5.** $P(1, \text{not } 1)$ **6.** $P(3, 3)$

_____ _____ _____

7. $P(\text{not } 1, 1)$ **8.** $P(0, 1)$ **9.** $P(1 \text{ or } 2, \text{not } 3)$

_____ _____ _____

47

Name _____

Intervention Lesson **L24**

Dependent Events (continued)

Players pick a letter from the bag without looking. They record it and put it back. Then they pick another letter in the same way. Find the probability of the following.

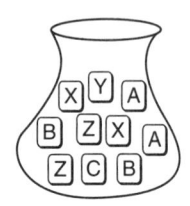

(Bag contains: X Y A B Z X A Z C B)

10. P(A, A)   **11.** P(X, Y)   **12.** P(A, not X)

_____   _____   _____

Players pick a letter from the bag without looking. They record it and do *not* put it back. Then they pick another letter in the same way. Find the probability of the following.

13. P(A, A)   **14.** P(X, Y)   **15.** P(A, not X)

_____   _____   _____

16. P(not A, not A)   **17.** P(B, not B)   **18.** P(vowel, Y)

_____   _____   _____

19. Math Reasoning If the probability of choosing a red tile is $\frac{2}{7}$, then what is the probability of choosing a red tile again if the first tile is not replaced?   _____

Test Prep Circle the correct letter for the answer.

20. The probability of choosing a 7 from a bag of cards is $\frac{3}{10}$. What is the probability of choosing a 7 and then a 7 again if the card is not replaced?

A $\frac{1}{15}$ **B** $\frac{6}{20}$ **C** $\frac{5}{19}$ **D** 1

Name _____

Intervention Lesson **L25**

Math Diagnosis and Intervention System

Making Line Plots

Example

A line plot shows how many times something happened.

How many goals were scored by the players?

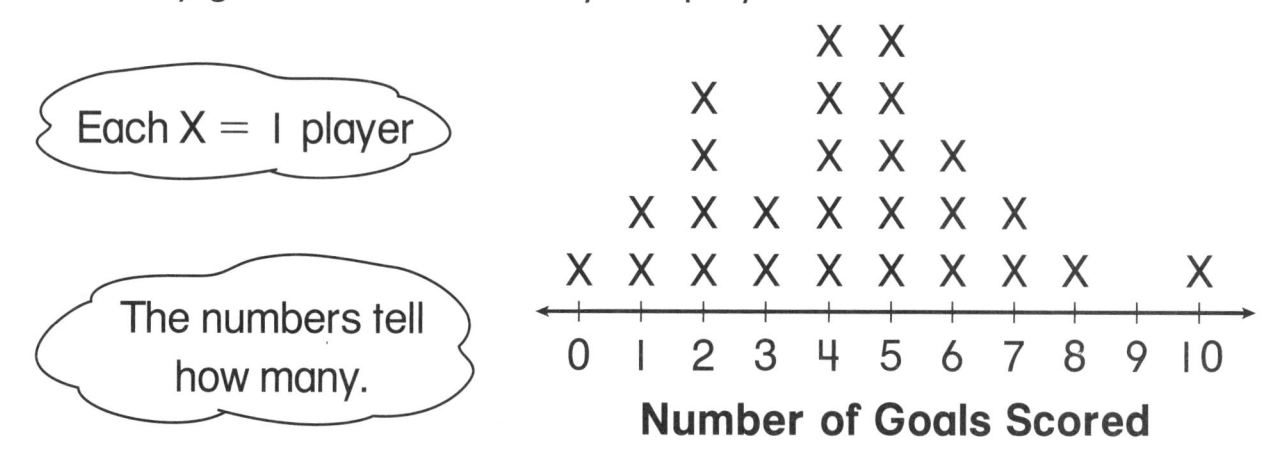

Each X = 1 player

The numbers tell how many.

```
                    X X
               X    X X
               X    X X X
         X X X X X X X
         X X X X X X X X X       X
        +-+-+-+-+-+-+-+-+-+-+-+
        0 1 2 3 4 5 6 7 8 9 10
```
Number of Goals Scored

Look: There are 3 Xs above the number 6.

The line plot shows that __3__ players have scored 6 goals.

Use the line plot to answer Questions 1–5.

1. How many players scored 4 goals? __5__ players

2. How many players scored 7 goals? _____ players

3. What was the most number of goals scored? _____ goals

4. How many players scored 2 or 3 goals? _____ players

5. Did more players score 7 or 8 goals? _____ goals

49

Name _____

Intervention Lesson **L25**

Making Line Plots (continued)

Some children made friendship bracelets.
The line plot shows how many bracelets each child made.

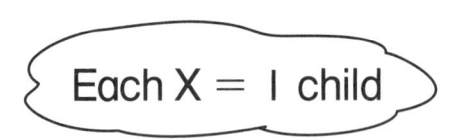

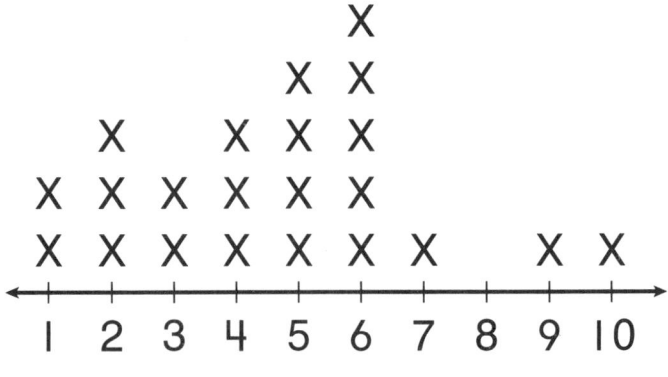

Each X = 1 child

```
                              X
                          X X
              X         X X X
    X X X X X X
    X X X X X X X         X X
    +-+-+-+-+-+-+-+-+-+-+
    1 2 3 4 5 6 7 8 9 10
```

Number of Bracelets Made

Use the line plot to answer Questions 6–9.

6. How many children made 4 bracelets? _____ children

7. What was the greatest number of bracelets made?
   _____ bracelets

8. How many children made 8 bracelets? _____ children

9. How many children made 3 or 4 bracelets?
   _____ children

10. **Writing in Math** Tell how you know how many children in all made bracelets?

   _____
   _____

Name _____

Intervention Lesson **L26**

Mean, Median, and Mode

Example

Find the mean, median, and mode of the data:

2, 7, 6, 4, 10, 7, 2, 2, 1, 2, 10, 7.

To find the *mean*, add the data together, then divide by the number of data.

$2 + 7 + 6 + 4 + 10 + 7 + 2 + 2 + 1 + 2 + 10 + 7 = 60$

$60 \div 12 = 5$

Five is the mean.

The *median* is the middle number when the data are listed in order. First list the data in order, then count to find the middle number(s).

1, 2, 2, 2, 2, 4, 6, 7, 7, 7, 10, 10

Since there are 2 middle numbers, the median is halfway in between them. Five is between 4 and 6 so the median is 5.

The *mode* is the number that occurs most often.

2 occurs four times, so the mode is 2.

Find the mean, median, and mode of each data set.

1. 2, 5, 1, 8, 8, 12, 6

mean _____

median _____

mode(s) _____

2. 25, 60, 20, 45, 25

mean _____

median _____

mode(s) _____

3. 15, 18, 12, 18, 14, 13

mean _____

median _____

mode(s) _____

4. 32, 36, 36, 32

mean _____

median _____

mode(s) _____

5. 54, 54, 60

mean _____

median _____

mode(s) _____

6. 2, 4, 7, 12, 17, 12, 2, 7, 3, 4

mean _____

median _____

mode(s) _____

51

Name _____

Math Diagnosis and Intervention System

Intervention Lesson **L26**

Mean, Median, and Mode (continued)

Find the mean, median, and mode of each data set.

7. 4, 1, 1, 8, 8, 12, 8

   mean _____

   median _____

   mode(s) _____

8. 35, 23, 15, 23

   mean _____

   median _____

   mode(s) _____

9. 15, 11, 12, 18, 14, 11, 9, 14

   mean _____

   median _____

   mode(s) _____

10. If the 12 in Problem 7 is changed to a 5, how does that affect the mean, median, and mode?

    _____

    _____

11. If an outlier of 100 is added to the data in Problem 8, how does that affect the mean, median, and mode?

    _____

    _____

12. **Math Reasoning** What is affected the most by an outlier—the mean, the median, or the mode?

    _____

Test Prep Circle the correct letter for the answer.

13. Find the median of the following data set: 4, 7, 1, 5, 0, 0, 6, 7

    A 5   **B** 4.5   **C** 2.5   **D** 0

14. Find the mode(s) of the following data set: 7, 5, 1, 12, 15, 5, 3, 3

    A 5   **B** 3   **C** 4   **D** 3 and 5

Finding Averages

Example

Find the mean of the data: $350, $210, $460, $740.

To find the *mean,* add the data together, then divide by the number of data.

$350 + $210 + $460 + $740 = $1,760
$1,760 ÷ 4 = $440
$440 is the mean.

Find the mean for each data set.

1. $120, $280, $410, $300, $180

2. 175 ft, 136 ft, 157 ft, 112 ft

3. 23 in., 37 in., 67 in., 93 in., 25 in.

4. 5,341 km, 6,780 km, 2,543 km

5. 89 weeks, 37 weeks, 27 weeks, 12 weeks, 86 weeks, 97 weeks

6. 3 runs, 5 runs, 8 runs, 4 runs, 10 runs, 5 runs, 4 runs, 1 run

7. $991, $759, $610, $967, $733

8. 36 lb, 53 lb, 25 lb, 14 lb

9. 76s, 36s, 98s, 25s, 38s, 27s

10. 1,664 books, 2,533 books, 1,267 books, 7,668 books

Name _____   Intervention Lesson **L27**

Math Diagnosis and Intervention System

Finding Averages (continued)

Find the mean for each data set.

11. 67%, 44%, 32%, 86%, 12%, 11%

12. 379 points, 255 points, 116 points

_____   _____

13. $1,561, $2,689, $1,442, $3,522, $1,756

14. 4 h, 1 h, 0 h, 5 h, 7 h, 0 h, 5 h, 2 h

_____   _____

15. Dale worked 7 days and made $350. What was the average amount he made each day?   _____

16. Mrs. Hernandez's math class made the following scores on a quiz: 5, 7, 8, 7, 9, 10, 2, 2, 3. If 2 points are added to everybody's score, how is the mean affected?

_____

17. Math Reasoning If a number is to be added to the data set in Exercise 11, what amount would affect the mean least? Explain.

_____

_____

Test Prep Circle the correct letter for the answer.

18. Find the mean of the following data set:
326, 442, 0, 876

  A 137   **B** 1,644   **C** 411   **D** 548

19. If a number is to be added to the following data set, which amount would affect the mean the least?
36, 64, 23, 117

  A 117   **B** 60   **C** 64   **D** 36

Name _____

Intervention Lesson **L28**

Stem-and-Leaf Plots

Example

Organize the data of the number of books sixth-grade students have read this semester in a stem-and-leaf plot:
6, 9, 34, 11, 22, 15, 40, 22, 47, 25, 22

Each stem stands for the first digit of each number.

Stem	Leaves
0	6 9
1	1 5
2	2 2 2 5
3	4
4	0 7

Each leaf stands for the second digit of each number.

Find the mean, median, and mode.

To find the *mean*, find the sum of all the numbers in the set of data:
6 + 9 + 11 + 15 + 22 + 22 + 22 + 25 + 34 + 40 + 47 = 253.
Then divide by the number of addends:
253 ÷ 11 = 23.
The mean is 23.

The *median* is the middle number of the set of data.
The median is 22.

The *mode* is the number that occurs most often in the set of data.
The mode is 22.

---

1. Organize the data below for the pounds of newspapers collected by the classes for recycling into a stem-and-leaf plot:
   6, 18, 12, 13, 11, 12, 12.

2. Find the mean of the data. _____

3. Find the range of the data. _____

4. Find the median of the data. _____

5. Find the mode(s) of the data. _____

55

Name _____

Intervention Lesson L28

Stem-and-Leaf Plots (continued)

6. Organize the following data for math scores of 6th grade students into a stem-and-leaf plot:

90, 88, 72, 69, 68, 76, 77, 88, 80, 82, 91, 91, 99, 84, 84, 78, 78.

7. Find the mean of the data. _____

8. Find the range of the data. _____

9. Find the median of the data. _____

10. Find the mode(s) of the data. _____

11. One of the students' scores has a 7 as a stem and an odd number as a leaf. Find that student's score. _____

12. Find the median of the scores if the 2 lowest scores are excluded. _____

13. Find the mode(s) of the scores if the 2 lowest scores are excluded. _____

14. Math Reasoning How do the 2 lowest scores affect the median and the mode? Explain.

_____

_____

Test Prep Circle the correct letter for the answer.

Stem	Leaves
0	0, 3, 4, 8
1	2, 8
2	0, 1, 1, 3

15. Find the median of the data in the stem-and-leaf diagram.

A 5   **B** 13   **C** 15   **D** 21

16. Find the mode of the data in the stem-and-leaf diagram.

A 0 and 1   **B** 13   **C** 15   **D** 21

56

Name _____

Intervention Lesson **L29**

Sampling Methods

Example

Tell whether the sample is likely to be representative or biased. Identify the method as random sampling, convenience sampling, or responses to a survey.

A person stands outside the local mall on a Saturday morning and asks those entering what is their favorite day to shop.

The sample is biased. Those persons entering on a Saturday will most likely choose Saturday as their favorite day.

The method is convenience sampling because it was convenient for the person to ask those entering the mall on Saturday morning.

Tell whether each sample is likely to be representative or biased. Explain your answers. Identify each as random sampling, convenience sampling, or responses to a survey.

1. A volunteer agency contacts every 20th agency in their directory to find out the number of hours volunteers work at their agency.

_____

_____

2. When students enroll at Jefferson Middle School, they are asked to tell their mode of transportation to school. The results are tallied.

_____

_____

Name _____

Intervention Lesson **L29**

Math Diagnosis and Intervention System

Sampling Methods (continued)

Tell whether each sample is likely to be representative or biased. Explain your answers. Identify each as random sampling, convenience sampling, or responses to a survey.

3. Raul is running for class president. He stands outside his classroom and asks students whom they plan to vote for.

_____
_____

4. To find out student's average grade points at his school, Ricky asked every 5th student on his school's roster to tell him their grade point average.

_____
_____

5. Byron has a jar of 500 marbles. He wants to know how many of them are blue. He takes a handful of the marbles as a sample and finds that 10 of the 50 marbles in the sample are blue and concludes that 20%, or 100 of the total jar, is blue. He later counts all the blue marbles and finds that 200 of them are blue. Was Byron's sample biased? What could have made it biased?

_____
_____

Test Prep Circle the correct letter for the answer.

6. Identify the method of sampling used: A newspaper asks readers to send in a questionnaire about community activities.

   A Random sampling   **C** Convenience sampling

   B Responses to a survey   **D** Representative sampling

Intervention Lesson **L30**

Frequency Tables and Line Plots

Example 1

The team manager recorded the number of goals scored in each of the last 15 soccer games.

0 1 2 1 0 1 1 3 2 1 3 1 2 2 6

A frequency table can be used to help organize and analyze data.

Goals	Tally	Frequency
0	||	2
1	⦀|	6
2	||||	4
3	||	2
6	|	1

Example 2

A line plot is another way to display data.

Some data is more spread out. The 6 is an outlier. Outliers effect the mean.

Find the mean. Then find the mean without the outlier.

```
X
X
X  X
X  X
X  X  X  X
X  X  X  X              X
0  1  2  3  4  5  6
```

$0 + 1 + 2 + 1 + 0 + 1 + 1 + 3 + 2 + 1 + 3 + 1 + 2 + 2 + \underline{6} = \frac{26}{15} = 1.73$

$0 + 1 + 2 + 1 + 0 + 1 + 1 + 3 + 2 + 1 + 3 + 1 + 2 + 2 = \frac{20}{14} = 1.43$

Members of Mrs. Jones's class recorded the number of students absent from their class on each day of a 10-day period.

1 0 1 0 0 2 2 3 8 1

1. Represent this data with a frequency table.

2. Represent this data with a line plot. Identify any outliers.

59

Name _____

Math Diagnosis and Intervention System

Intervention Lesson **L30**

Frequency Tables and Line Plots (continued)

Mr. Sun recorded his student's scores on the last quiz.

7 8 9 10 8 10 9 8 9 10 9 7 8 9 10 8 9 7 10 7

3. Represent the data with a frequency table.

_____

4. Represent the data with a line plot.

5. Compute the range, median, mode, and mean of the data set.

_____

6. The team manager recorded the number of points John made in the last 12 basketball games.

0 2 18 22 24 20 18 16 18 20 22 18

Compute the range, median, mode, and mean of the data set.

_____

Test Prep Circle the correct letter for the answer.

7. Given the data set 72, 75, 73, 71, 70, 50, and 76, which of the numbers is an outlier?

   A 76   **B** 75   **C** 72   **D** 50

Name _____

Intervention Lesson **L31**

Misleading Graphs

Example

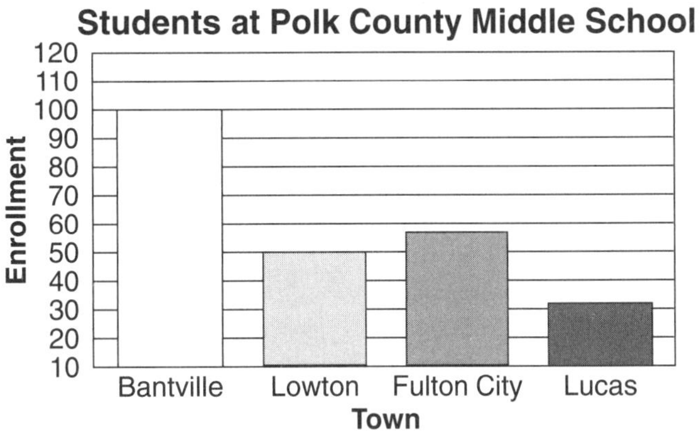

Marcel saw this graph in the newspaper and made this claim:

According to the enrollment forms, more than two times as many students at Polk County Middle School live in Bantville than Lowton.

Is this an accurate claim?

The bar for Bantville is more than twice as tall as that for Lowton, but when reading the y-axis, it is seen that Bantville has 100 students and Lowton has 50 students.

Because 100 is exactly two times 50, the claim of having more than two times as many students is incorrect.

Explain why the claim is misleading.

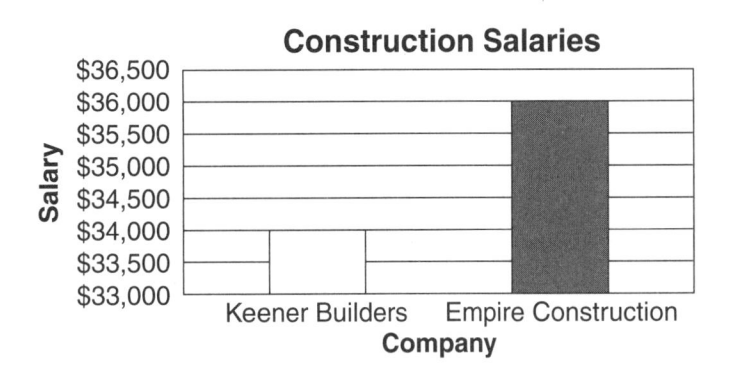

1. Empire Construction claims that their employees are paid more than three times what Keener Builders pays its employees. Is this claim correct? Explain.

_____
_____
_____
_____
_____

61

Name _____ Intervention Lesson **L31**

Misleading Graphs (continued)

Explain why the claim is misleading.

2. According to a recent survey, consumers greatly prefer Sudsy shampoo.

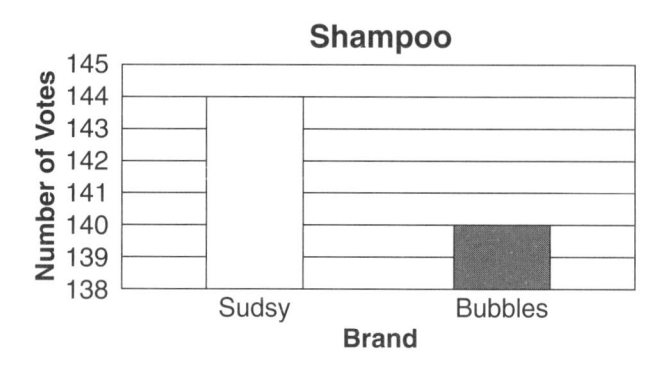

Shampoo bar graph: y-axis "Number of Votes" ranges from 138 to 145. Sudsy bar at 145, Bubbles bar at 140. x-axis "Brand".

_____

_____

_____

Test Prep Circle the correct letter for the answer.

3. The cost of cat food has risen slower than the price of dog food. Why is this claim incorrect?

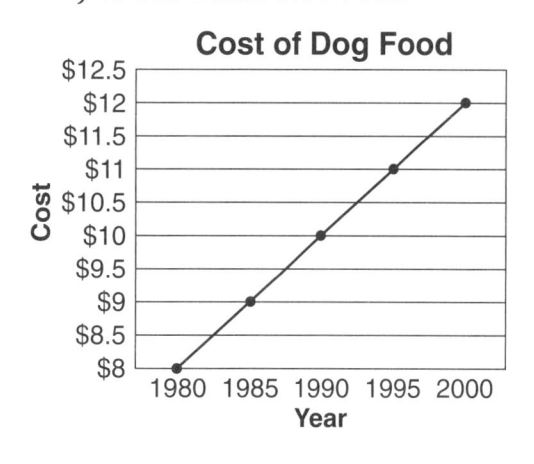

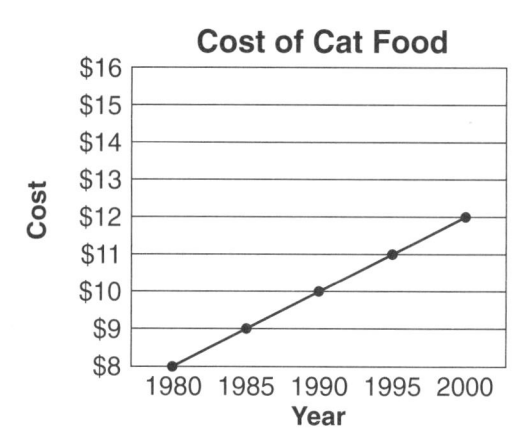

Cost of Dog Food: y-axis "Cost" from $8 to $12.5; 1980=$8, 1985=$9, 1990=$10, 1995=$11, 2000=$12. x-axis "Year".

Cost of Cat Food: y-axis "Cost" from $8 to $16; 1980=$8, 1985=$9, 1990=$10, 1995=$11, 2000=$12. x-axis "Year".

- **A** The years used for the x-axis are different for dog food than for cat food.
- **B** The y-axis scales for costs are different for dog food than for cat food.
- **C** The costs do not begin in the same year.
- **D** The scales for the x-axis and y-axis should be reversed.

Name _____

Math Diagnosis and Intervention System

Intervention Practice **L1**

Recording Data from a Survey

Fill in the ○ for the correct answer.

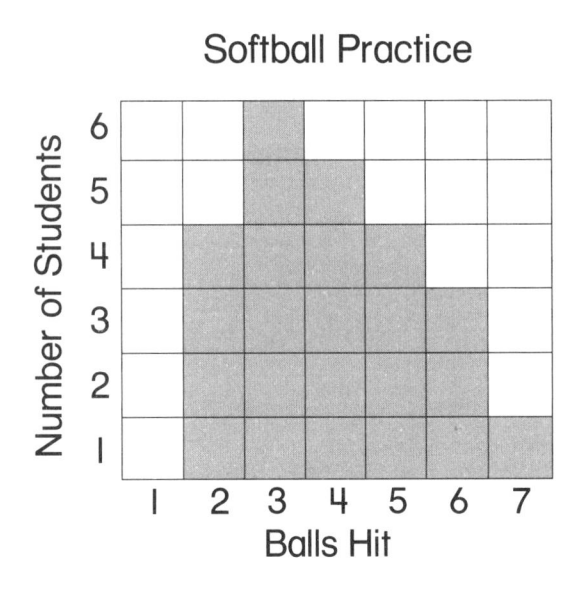

Softball Practice

(Bar graph: Number of Students vs. Balls Hit. Bars: 1 ball = 0, 2 balls = 4, 3 balls = 6, 4 balls = 5, 5 balls = 4, 6 balls = 3, 7 balls = 1)

1. What was the greatest number of balls hit?

    7 balls   6 balls   4 balls   3 balls
      ○   ○   ○   ○

2. What was the fewest number of balls hit?

    1 ball   2 balls   3 balls   4 balls
      ○   ○   ○   ○

3. What is the difference between the greatest and fewest balls hit?

      2   4   5   6
      ○   ○   ○   ○

63

Reading and Making Pictographs

Circle the correct letter for the answer.

Use the pictograph to answer Questions 1–4.

Our Favorite Fruit

bananas	👤👤👤👤
apples	👤👤👤👤👤👤👤
pears	👤⸺
oranges	👤👤👤👤👤

Key: 👤 = 2 children

1. How many children chose oranges as their favorite fruit?
   - A 10
   - B 7
   - C 5
   - D 4

2. Which fruit was chosen the least?
   - A bananas
   - B apples
   - C oranges
   - D pears

3. How many more children chose apples than oranges?
   - A 3
   - B 4
   - C 9
   - D 5

4. How many children all together chose bananas and pears?
   - A 12
   - B 11
   - C 10
   - D 9

Use the pictograph to answer Questions 5–8.

Number of Trees in the National Park

Oak	🌳🌳🌳
Pine	🌳🌳🌳🌳🌳🌳
Ash	🌳🌳🌳🌳🌳
Maple	🌳🌳🌳🌳🌳🌳🌳

Key: 🌳 = 5 trees

5. How many ash trees are in the park?
   - A 15
   - B 20
   - C 25
   - D 35

6. How many more maple trees are there than pine trees?
   - A 5
   - B 10
   - C 20
   - D 25

7. How many oak and pine trees are there all together?
   - A 40
   - B 45
   - C 50
   - D 60

8. Of which tree is there the least number in the park?
   - A Pine
   - B Oak
   - C Ash
   - D Maple

Reading and Making a Bar Graph

Circle the correct letter for the answer.

Leonard is using the data in the table to make a bar graph. Use the data in the table and the partially completed graph to answer Questions 1–3.

Color	Votes	Color	Votes
Red	5	Orange	2
Blue	6	Green	4
Yellow	3	Purple	5

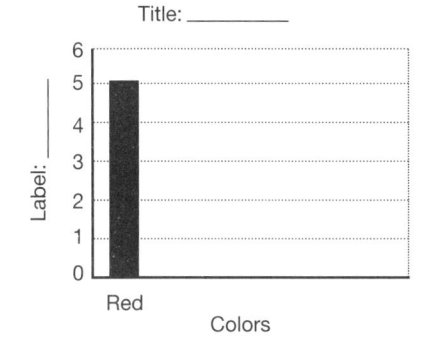

1. Which color will get the tallest bar?
   - A Blue
   - B Purple
   - C Red
   - D Yellow

2. Which two colors will have bars of the same length?
   - A Blue and Red
   - B Green and Yellow
   - C Purple and Green
   - D Red and Purple

3. Which of these would be used for the label on the left side of the graph?
   - A Favorite Colors
   - B Number of Votes
   - C Month of the Year
   - D Length

4. A scientist at a national park counted the animals she saw. The scientist made the bar graph shown below.

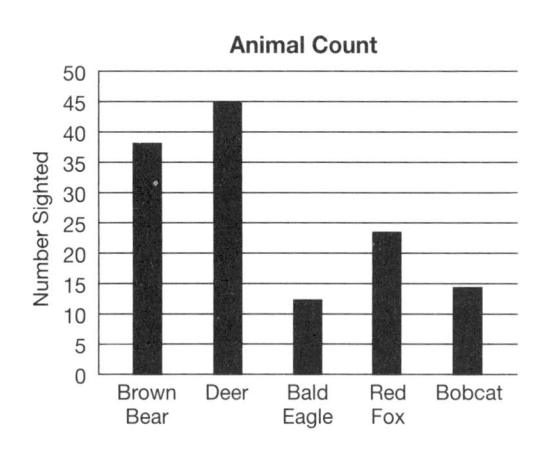

   Which was sighted more than 15 times, but less than 35 times?
   - A Deer
   - B Bobcat
   - C Bald Eagle
   - D Red Fox

65

Name _____

Intervention Practice **L4**

Math Diagnosis and Intervention System

Graphing Ordered Pairs

Circle the correct letter for the answer.

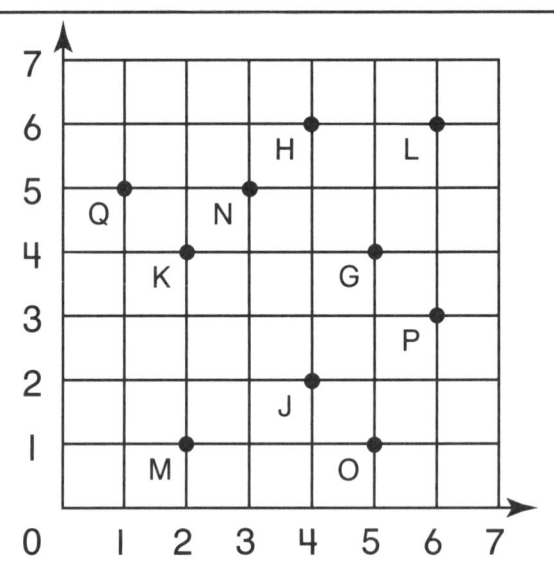

Find the ordered pair that names the location of each point.

1. K
   - **A** (6, 6)
   - **B** (5, 1)
   - **C** (2, 4)
   - **D** (3, 5)

2. P
   - **A** (6, 3)
   - **B** (6, 6)
   - **C** (4, 2)
   - **D** (2, 1)

3. O
   - **A** (4, 2)
   - **B** (5, 1)
   - **C** (6, 3)
   - **D** (3, 5)

4. G
   - **A** (4, 2)
   - **B** (5, 4)
   - **C** (6, 3)
   - **D** (3, 5)

Give the letter of the point named by each ordered pair.

5. (6, 6)
   - **A** P
   - **B** N
   - **C** Q
   - **D** L

6. (1, 5)
   - **A** K
   - **B** M
   - **C** Q
   - **D** N

7. (2, 1)
   - **A** O
   - **B** M
   - **C** J
   - **D** P

8. (3, 5)
   - **A** G
   - **B** P
   - **C** N
   - **D** O

66

Name _____

Intervention Practice **L5**

Reading and Making Line Graphs

Circle the correct letter for the answer.

The graph shows the number of eggs produced in the first six months of one year. Use the graph for Questions 1–3.

Monthly Egg Production

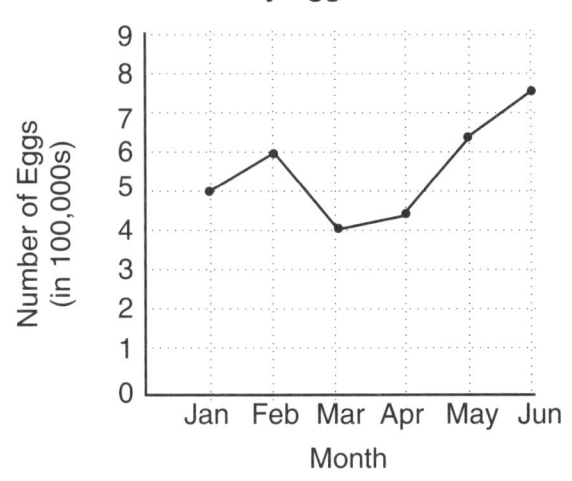

1. What scale is used on this graph?

   A 1
   B 100
   C 10,000
   D 100,000

2. What was the total number of eggs produced in February?

   A 500,000
   B 600,000
   C 700,000
   D 800,000

3. During which month were 400,000 eggs produced?

   A June
   B May
   C March
   D February

4. Which is the best scale for making a line graph of the data?

Number of Fifth-Grade Students	
Year	Number
1997	78
1998	84
1999	91
2000	97

   A 1 student per unit
   B 5 students per unit
   C 20 students per unit
   D 50 students per unit

Use the line graph for Questions 5 and 6.

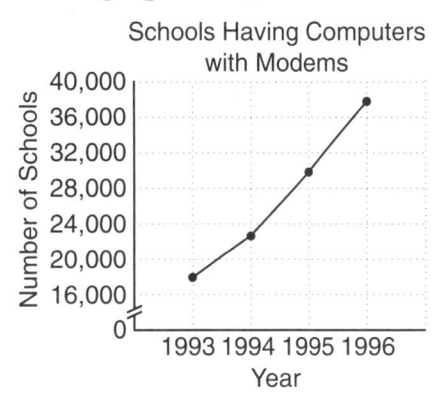

Schools Having Computers with Modems

5. How many schools had computers with modems in 1996?

   A 23,000
   B 31,000
   C 38,000
   D 52,000

6. In what year did 23,000 schools have computers with modems?

   A 1993
   B 1994
   C 1995
   D 1996

67

Intervention Practice **L6**

Choosing Appropriate Graphs

Circle the correct letter for the answer.

1. Choose an appropriate graph to display the data.

Year	Population
1970	12,000,000
1980	13,750,000
1990	15,250,000
2000	18,790,000

   A Pictograph   C Line graph
   B Line plot   D Circle graph

2. Which type of display is NOT a good choice to show the data.

Month	Number of Gallons of Ice Cream Sold
June	70
July	110
August	150
September	180

   A Pictograph
   B Stem-and-Leaf Plot
   C Bar Graph
   D Line Plot

3. Choose an appropriate display for the favorite activities of children at summer camp.

   A Bar graph   C Circle graph
   B Line graph   D Pictograph

Use the graph below for Questions 4–6.

Favorite Lunch Sandwich	
Peanut Butter	🥪🥪🥪
Ham	🥪🥪🥪🥪
Turkey	🥪
Peanut Butter and Jelly	🥪🥪🥪🥪🥪

🥪 = 3

4. How many students were surveyed?

   A 13   B 26   C 39   D 54

5. How many more students prefer ham to turkey?

   A 3   B 9   C 12   D 15

6. Which other type of graph could have been used to display the data?

   A Line graph
   B Circle graph
   C Bar graph
   D Stem-and-leaf plot

Circle Graphs

Circle the correct letter for the answer.

Use the circle graph for Questions 1–3.

Daily Activities

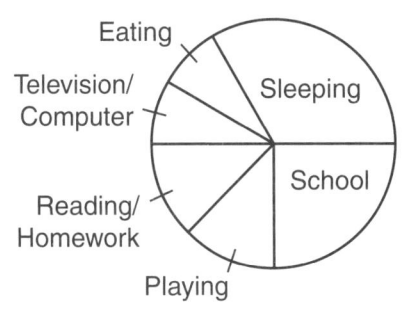

1. What fraction does eating represent in the circle graph?

   A $\frac{1}{6}$ C $\frac{1}{12}$

   B $\frac{1}{8}$ D $\frac{1}{15}$

2. What sector represents $\frac{1}{3}$ of the circle graph?

   A school   C play
   B sleeping D other

3. Which sector represents $\frac{1}{4}$ of the circle graph?

   A reading/homework
   B sleeping
   C television/computer
   D school

Use the chart for Questions 4–6.

| What Cassandra Spent on a Shopping Trip ||
Item	Amount $
Boots	$64
Turtleneck	$14
Sweater	$40
Socks	$10
Jeans	$32

4. In a circle graph of the data, which sector would be the smallest?

   A boots   C socks
   B jeans   D turtleneck

5. What sector would be twice as large as the sector for jeans?

   A boots   C sweater
   B turtleneck D socks

6. What is the total amount of money spent?

   A $120   C $150
   B $140   D $160

Name _____

Intervention Practice **L8**

Double Bar Graphs

Choose the correct letter for the answer.

Use the table for Questions 1 and 2.

Boxes of Cookies Sold

	Amy	Tiffany
Sunday	50	75
Monday	25	30
Tuesday	15	20
Wednesday	30	15
Thursday	30	30
Friday	70	50
Saturday	45	100

1. Suppose you are going to use the data in the table to make a double bar graph showing each amount represented. Which labels should you use for the axes?

    A Amy and Tiffany
    B Girls and Days
    C Number of Boxes and Girls
    D Number of Boxes and Days

2. Which size interval would be best to use for the boxes of cookies?

    A 2
    B 10
    C 50
    D 100

Use the bar graph for Questions 3 and 4.

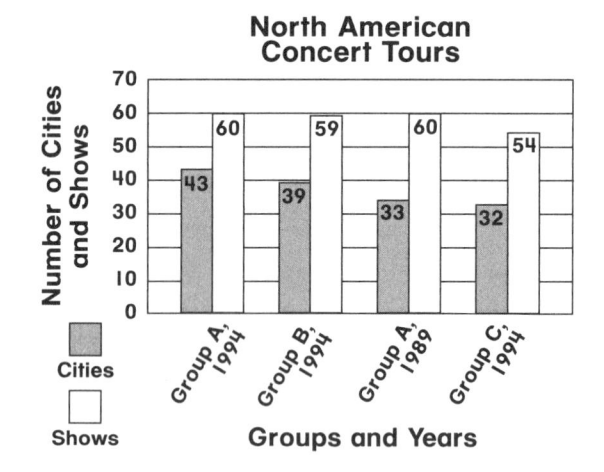

North American Concert Tours

(Bar graph showing Number of Cities and Shows for Groups and Years: Group A, 1994: 43 cities, 60 shows; Group B, 1994: 39 cities, 59 shows; Group A, 1989: 33 cities, 60 shows; Group C, 1994: 32 cities, 54 shows.)

3. What does the horizontal axis on the graph represent?

    A The group name and the tour year.
    B The number of cities and shows.
    C The number of tours.
    D The number of cities.

4. Which tour showed the greatest difference between the number of cities visited and the number of shows played?

    A Group A, 1994
    B Group B, 1994
    C Group C, 1994
    D Group A, 1989

Intervention Practice **L9**

Scatterplots

Circle the correct letter for the answer.

1. What does the scatterplot show?

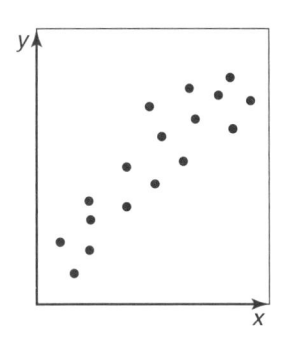

   A positive trend
   B negative trend
   C no trend
   D positive then negative trend

2. Which statement is true about the scatterplot?

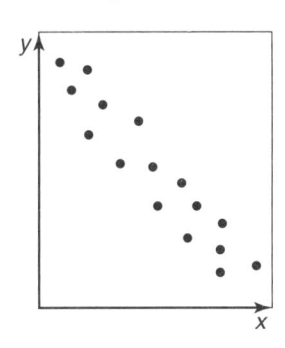

   A The points show no trend between the two sets of data.
   B As the values of one set of data increase, the values of the other set increase.
   C As the values of one set of data increase, the values of the other set of data decrease.
   D The points show a positive trend.

3. Which sets of data would most likely have a negative trend?

   A The height of a person and that person's shoe size.
   B The age of a car and its selling price.
   C The day of the month and the temperature outside.
   D The population of a state and the number of governors.

4. The scatterplot below shows the relationship between two sets of data. Which of the following statements is true?

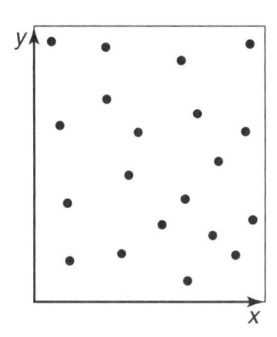

   A The points show no trend between the two sets of data.
   B As the values of one set of data increase, the values of the other set increase.
   C As the values of one set of data decrease, the values of the other set increase.
   D The plotted points show a positive trend between the data sets.

71

Understanding Probability

Circle the correct letter for the answer.

Members of the Sky Blue Club wrote their names on cards. Use the names on the cards to answer Questions 1–3.

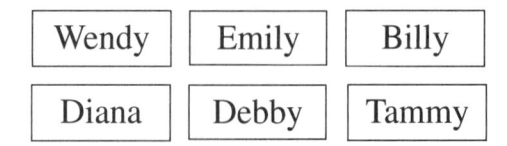

| Wendy | Emily | Billy |
| Diana | Debby | Tammy |

1. If you choose one of the cards without looking, what is the likelihood that you will get a card with a name that has 5 letters?

   A Impossible   **C** Likely
   B Unlikely   **D** Certain

2. If you choose one of the cards without looking, what is the likelihood that you will get a card with a boy's name?

   A Equally likely as unlikely   **C** Certain
   B Unlikely   **D** Likely

3. If you choose one card without looking, what is the likelihood that you will get a card with a name that ends in *y*?

   A Equally likely as unlikely   **C** Likely
   B Unlikely   **D** Certain

4. Which of the following events is unlikely?

   A Tomorrow the sun will shine.
   B There will be shows on television tonight.
   C Tomorrow you will eat lunch at 4:00 A.M.
   D The wind will blow outside tonight.

5. Which of the following events is certain?

   A It will rain tomorrow.
   B You will eat breakfast at 8:00 A.M.
   C Tuesday will come after Monday next week.
   D You will go to school on Wednesday.

6. Which of the following events is likely?

   A It will snow in June.
   B The sun will rise in the south.
   C An ice cube left at room temperature will melt.
   D You will eat dinner at 1:00 A.M.

Intervention Practice **L11**

Fair and Unfair

Circle the correct letter for the answer.

1. What is the chance that the spinner will land on K?

   2 out of _____

   A 1   C 3
   B 6   D 2

Use the Spinner M to answer Questions 2–5.

Spinner M

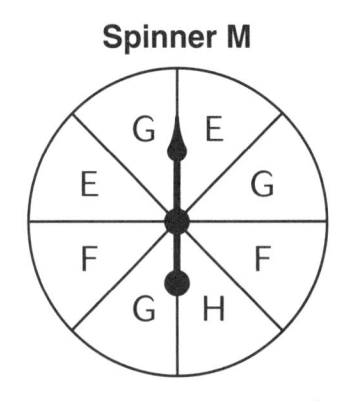

2. What is the chance that the spinner will land on F?

   A 2 out of 8   C 3 out of 8
   B 2 out of 4   D 1 out of 8

3. What is the chance that the spinner will land on H?

   A 2 out of 6   C 2 out of 8
   B 1 out of 4   D 1 out of 8

4. What is the chance that the spinner will land on G?

   A 1 out of 8   C 3 out of 8
   B 2 out of 8   D 3 out of 4

5. What is the chance that the spinner will land on E?

   A 3 out of 8   C 1 out of 8
   B 2 out of 4   D 2 out of 8

6. What is the chance that Spinner X will land on K?

   Spinner X

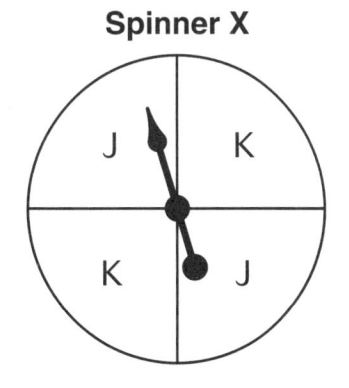

   2 out of _____

   A 1   C 2
   B 4   D 6

73

Name _____

Intervention Practice **L12**

Finding Probability

Circle the correct letter for the answer.

Use the spinner for Questions 1–3.

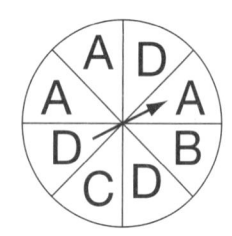

1. Give the probability of spinning a D on this spinner.
   A $\frac{1}{2}$
   B $\frac{3}{8}$
   C $\frac{1}{3}$
   D $\frac{1}{4}$

2. What is the probability that you would spin a C on this spinner?
   A $\frac{1}{8}$
   B $\frac{1}{6}$
   C $\frac{1}{4}$
   D $\frac{1}{3}$

3. Which of these shows the probability of spinning an E on this spinner?
   A 1
   B $\frac{1}{2}$
   C $\frac{1}{8}$
   D 0

4. A bag contains 5 red marbles, 3 blue marbles, and 2 purple marbles. What is the probability of getting a blue marble if you reach in and take one without looking?
   A $\frac{3}{10}$
   C $\frac{3}{7}$
   B $\frac{1}{2}$
   D $\frac{3}{5}$

5. You toss a number cube with one of the numbers 1, 2, 3, 4, 5, or 6 on each of the sides. What is the likelihood that you will toss an even number?
   A Equally likely as unlikely
   B Impossible
   C Likely
   D Unlikely

6. What is the probability of spinning a 1?

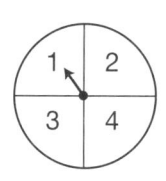

   A 0
   C $\frac{1}{2}$
   B $\frac{1}{6}$
   D $\frac{1}{4}$

74

Understanding Probability

Circle the correct letter for the answer.

These drink cartons are on a tray.
Use the drink cartons to answer Questions 1–4.

1. You are randomly given 1 drink carton. What is the likelihood that you will get grape juice?

    A Certain
    B Impossible
    C Unlikely
    D Equally likely as unlikely

2. You are randomly given 1 drink carton. What is the least likely choice?

    A Orange juice
    B Apple juice
    C Chocolate milk
    D White milk

3. You are randomly given 1 drink carton. What is the likelihood that you will get apple juice?

    A Certain
    B Impossible
    C Likely
    D Unlikely

4. You are randomly given 1 drink carton. What is the likelihood that you will get milk?

    A Certain
    B Likely
    C Impossible
    D Equally likely as unlikely

5. You toss a number cube with one of the numbers 1, 2, 3, 4, 5, or 6 on each of the sides. What is the likelihood that you will toss a 1?

    A Certain
    B Equally likely as unlikely
    C Likely
    D Unlikely

6. You toss the number cube in Question 5. What is the likelihood that you will toss a 0?

    A Equally likely as unlikely
    B Impossible
    C Unlikely
    D Certain

Listing Outcomes

Circle the correct letter for the answer.

The shapes below are each drawn on one of eight index cards. The cards are placed in 3 bags, one for crayons, one for fruit, and one for geometric figures.

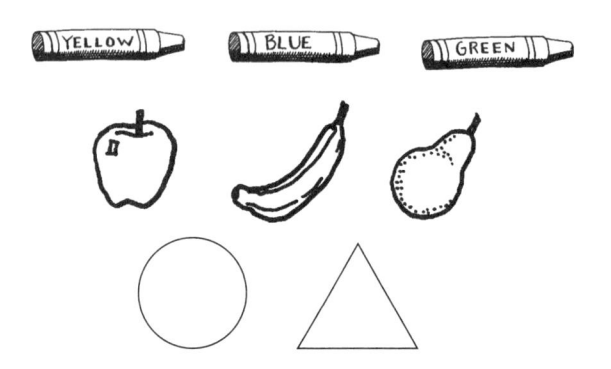

1. How many possible outcomes are there of picking a crayon and a geometric figure?

   A 2   C 6
   B 3   D 9

2. Which list shows all the possible outcomes of spinning both spinners together?

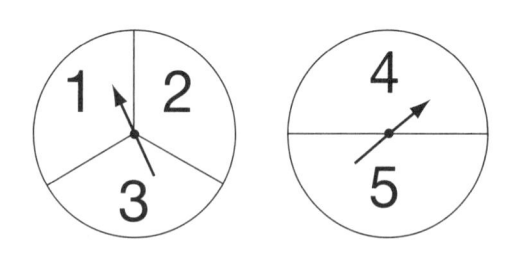

   A 1, 4; 1, 5; 2, 4; 2, 5; 3, 4; 3, 5
   B 1, 1; 4, 4; 3, 5
   C 1, 1; 2, 2; 3, 3
   D 2, 2; 4, 4

3. Which list shows all the possible outcomes of spinning both spinners together?

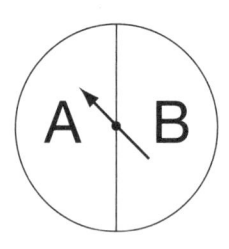

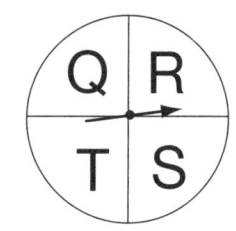

   A AQ, AR, AS, AT
   B BQ, BR, BS, BT
   C AB, AQ, AR, AS, AT, BA, BQ, BR, BS, BT
   D AQ, AR, AS, AT, BQ, BR, BS, BT

4. Which list shows all the possible outcomes of spinning both spinners together?

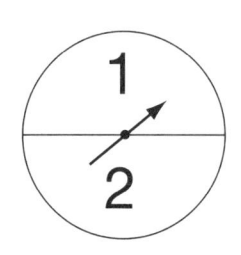

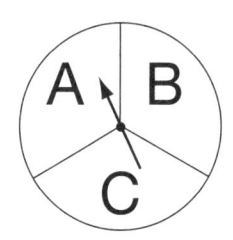

   A A, 1; B, 1; C, 1
   B A, 1; A, 2; B, 1; B, 2; C, 1; C, 2
   C A, A; B, B; C, C
   D 1, 1; 2, 2; A, A; B, B; C, C

Name _____

Intervention Practice L15

Displaying Probability Data and Making Predictions

Circle the correct letter for the answer.

The students visiting South Padre Island chose their favorite activity on the island. They made a graph to show the results.

Use the graph to answer Questions 1 and 2.

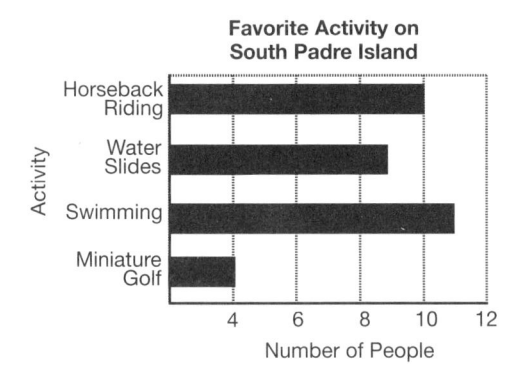

Favorite Activity on South Padre Island

1. Which activity was chosen by the most students?

   A Horseback riding
   B Miniature golf
   C Swimming
   D Water slides

2. In all, how many students voted for their favorite activity?

   A 11 students
   B 24 students
   C 30 students
   D 34 students

This bar graph shows the number of animals sighted in a park for one month.

Use the graph to answer Questions 3 and 4.

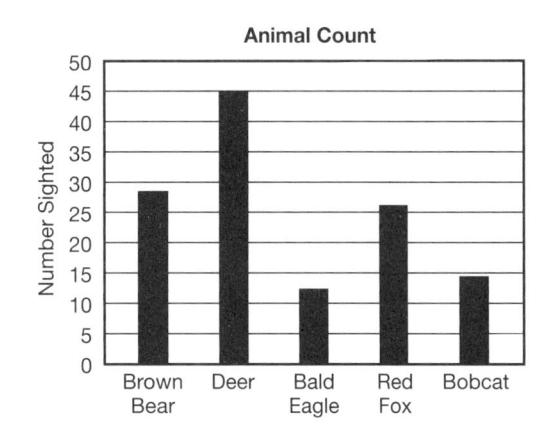

Animal Count

3. Which animal was sighted the least?

   A Brown Bear
   B Red Fox
   C Deer
   D Bald Eagle

4. Which animals were sighted fewer than 25 times?

   A Brown Bear, Deer, Red Fox
   B Bald Eagle, Red Fox
   C Bald Eagle, Bobcat
   D Bald Eagle, Red Fox, Bobcat

Name _____

Intervention Practice **L16**

Predictions and Probability

Circle the correct letter for the answer.

1. A bag contains 8 blue marbles, 2 green marbles, and 2 red marbles. If you draw one marble, describe the chance of drawing a blue marble.

   A   Certain   C   Unlikely
   B   Impossible   D   Likely

Use the spinner for Questions 2–7.

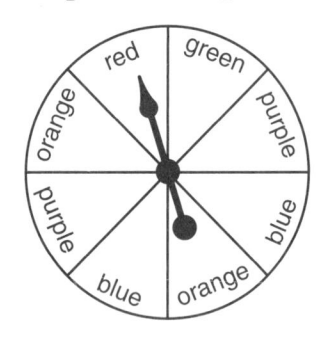

2. What are the chances of spinning green?

   A   Certain   C   Unlikely
   B   Impossible   D   Likely

3. Compare the chances of spinning purple or blue.

   A   Purple is more likely
   B   Blue is more likely
   C   Both are impossible
   D   Both are equally likely

4. What are the chances of spinning black?

   A   Certain   C   Unlikely
   B   Impossible   D   Likely

5. What are the chances of spinning red, green, orange, purple, or blue?

   A   Certain   C   Unlikely
   B   Impossible   D   Likely

6. What are the chances of spinning either blue, purple, or orange?

   A   Certain   C   Unlikely
   B   Impossible   D   Likely

7. Suppose the spinner is spun 80 times. How many times would you expect blue to be spun?

   A   2   C   10
   B   8   D   20

8. A number cube has sides labeled A, B, C, D, E, and F. Compare the chances of tossing a vowel with the chances of tossing a consonant.

   A   Tossing a vowel is less likely than tossing a consonant.
   B   Tossing a vowel and tossing a consonant are equally likely.
   C   Tossing a consonant is less likely than tossing a vowel.
   D   Tossing a vowel is more likely than tossing a consonant.

Name _____

Intervention Practice **L17**

Predicting Outcomes

Circle the correct letter for the answer.

Sally tossed 5 coins 70 times. The table shows the outcomes.
Use the table for Questions 1–3.

5 heads			
4 heads, 1 tail	⊔⊔⊔ ⊔⊔⊔	
3 heads, 2 tails	⊔⊔⊔ ⊔⊔⊔		
2 heads, 3 tails	⊔⊔⊔ ⊔⊔⊔ ⊔⊔⊔ ⊔⊔⊔ ⊔⊔⊔			
1 head, 4 tails	⊔⊔⊔ ⊔⊔⊔
5 tails	⊔⊔⊔	

1. To win the game, you must predict the next outcome correctly. Based on the previous results, which should you choose?

    A 4 heads, 1 tail
    B 3 heads, 2 tails
    C 2 heads, 3 tails
    D 1 head, 4 tails

2. The rules of the game are changed. You now win the game by predicting the outcome that is least likely to happen. Based on the previous results, which should you choose?

    A 5 heads **C** 1 head, 4 tails
    B 4 heads, 1 tail **D** 5 tails

3. If 4 coins are tossed, which of these results is not a possible outcome?

    A 4 heads
    B 3 heads, 1 tail
    C 2 heads, 3 tails
    D 4 tails

In another game, 3 two-colored counters were tossed 100 times. The table shows the outcomes.
Use the table for Questions 4–6.

3 red	⊔⊔⊔ ⊔⊔⊔				
2 red, 1 yellow	⊔⊔⊔ ⊔⊔⊔ ⊔⊔⊔ ⊔⊔⊔ ⊔⊔⊔ ⊔⊔⊔ ⊔⊔⊔ ⊔⊔⊔ ⊔⊔⊔				
1 red, 2 yellow	⊔⊔⊔ ⊔⊔⊔ ⊔⊔⊔ ⊔⊔⊔ ⊔⊔⊔		
3 yellow	⊔⊔⊔ ⊔⊔⊔

4. To win the game, you must predict the next outcome correctly. Based on the previous results, which should you choose?

    A 3 red **C** 1 red, 2 yellow
    B 2 red, 1 yellow **D** 3 yellow

5. The rules of the game are changed. You now win the game by predicting the outcome that is least likely to happen. Based on the previous results, which should you choose?

    A 3 red **C** 1 red, 2 yellow
    B 2 red, 1 yellow **D** 3 yellow

6. What is the probability that the toss will result in 3 yellow?

    A $\frac{1}{100}$ **C** 10
    B $\frac{27}{100}$ **D** $\frac{1}{10}$

79

Intervention Practice **L18**

Finding Probability

Circle the correct letter for the answer.

Use the spinner for Questions 1–3.

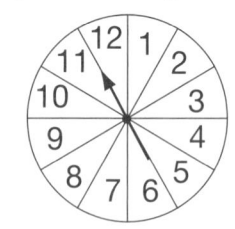

1. Give the probability of spinning an even number on this spinner.

   A 0
   B $\frac{1}{3}$
   C $\frac{5}{12}$
   D $\frac{1}{2}$

2. What is the probability of spinning a number from 1 to 12 on this spinner?

   A 0
   B $\frac{1}{12}$
   C $\frac{1}{2}$
   D 1

3. What is the probability of spinning a 3 on this spinner?

   A 1
   B $\frac{1}{4}$
   C $\frac{1}{6}$
   D $\frac{1}{12}$

4. There are 14 red apples and 12 green apples in a bag. If an apple is chosen at random, what is the probability that it will be red?

   A $\frac{6}{13}$ C $\frac{7}{13}$
   B $\frac{1}{2}$ D $\frac{7}{6}$

5. There are 6 blue beads and 9 green beads in a case. What is the probability of choosing a blue bead from the case at random?

   A $\frac{1}{6}$ C $\frac{2}{5}$
   B $\frac{2}{1}$ D $\frac{3}{2}$

6. Alice and Iris are tossing a number cube with the numbers 1 through 6. Alice gets a point if the number is even. Iris gets a point if the number is greater than 4. Which statement is NOT true about this game?

   A The probability of Iris getting a point is $\frac{1}{3}$, or about 33%.
   B Alice has a higher probability of winning than Iris does.
   C Alice has a lower probability of winning than Iris does.
   D Alice gets a point if she tosses a 2, 4, or 6.

Name _____

Intervention Practice **L19**

Counting Methods

Circle the correct letter for the answer.

Use this information for Questions 1–3.
You choose one card, replace it, and then choose another at random from cards A, B, C, D, and E.
Make a tree diagram for Questions 1 and 3.

1. Which ratio gives the probability of choosing two consonants?

   A $\frac{16}{25}$

   B $\frac{9}{25}$

   C $\frac{12}{16}$

   D $\frac{6}{20}$

2. Which ratio gives the probability of choosing a vowel and a consonant?

   A $\frac{10}{25}$

   B $\frac{6}{25}$

   C $\frac{8}{12}$

   D $\frac{5}{25}$

3. $P(E, C) =$

   A $\frac{2}{20}$

   B $\frac{1}{20}$

   C $\frac{1}{25}$

   D $\frac{2}{25}$

4. A spinner has 6 possible outcomes, the numbers 1 to 6. A second spinner has 3 possible outcomes, red, blue, and green. How many possible outcomes are there if you spin both spinners?

   A 24   C 12
   B 18   D 9

A pizza can have one of two different crusts and one of four different toppings as shown in the table. Use a tree diagram for Questions 5 and 6.

Crust	Toppings
thin	cheese
pan	pepperoni
	sausage
	vegetables

5. How many different pizzas are possible?

   A 4   C 16
   B 8   D 32

6. $P(\text{pan, sausage}) =$

   A $\frac{1}{16}$ C $\frac{2}{8}$

   B $\frac{1}{8}$ D $\frac{2}{4}$

81

Permutations and Combinations

Circle the correct letter for the answer.

1. Choose the situation in which order matters.

   A Choose 5 children to sing a song.

   B Choose 8 children to walk single file in a line from tallest to shortest.

   C Choose 5 charities to support.

   D Choose 3 fruits for a salad.

2. Choose the situation in which order does not matter.

   A Put 5 books on a shelf alphabetically by author.

   B Choose players for a batting lineup.

   C Choose roles for actors as they appear in the play.

   D Choose friends to invite to a party.

3. Bob launches two rockets. He has four different colors to choose from. How many different ways can he launch his rockets if the order matters?

   A 12   **C** 4
   B 6   **D** 2

4. In Question 3, how many different ways can he launch two rockets at once?

   A 12   **C** 4
   B 6   **D** 2

5. There are 6 class officers. How many ways can 2 of these students be selected to serve on a committee?

   A 30
   B 15
   C 60
   D 12

6. How many ways can you choose 3 flowers from 7?

   A 35
   B 21
   C 210
   D 24

7. Four marchers are deciding in what order to line up for a parade. In how many ways can they line up?

   A 28 ways
   B 24 ways
   C 22 ways
   D 6 ways

Name _____

Intervention Practice **L21**

Representing Probability

Circle the correct letter for the answer.

This spinner is used to determine the prize for each contest winner. Each winner receives the amount he or she spins.
Use the spinner for Questions 1–3.

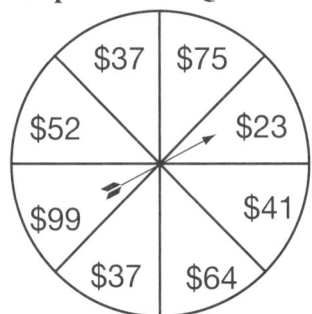

Spinner sections: $37, $75, $52, $23, $99, $41, $37, $64

1. What is the probability of spinning an odd number of dollars in one spin?

   A 12.5%
   B 37.5%
   C 50%
   D 75%

2. What is the probability of spinning more than $100 in one spin?

   A 1
   B 0.5
   C 0.25
   D 0

3. What is the probability that you will be awarded less than $50 on one spin in this game?

   A 10%   **C** 75%
   B 50%   **D** 62.5%

4. Raquel wanted to pick a red apple from the basket of apples because people who picked red apples would win a prize. The probability of winning a prize is 3 in 16. What is the probability that she will not pick a red apple?

   A 0.1875
   B 0.3125
   C 0.5
   D 0.8125

A bag contains 25 cards numbered 1 to 25. You pick a card at random. After you pick a card, you return it to the bag. Use this information for Questions 5 and 6.

5. What is the probability of picking a 4?

   A 40%
   B 4%
   C 16%
   D 1

6. What is the probability of picking an even number?

   A 0.5
   B 0.923
   C 0.48
   D 0.52

83

Name _____

Intervention Practice **L22**

Math Diagnosis and Intervention System

Adding Probabilities

Circle the correct letter for the answer.

Use the spinner for Questions 1–3.

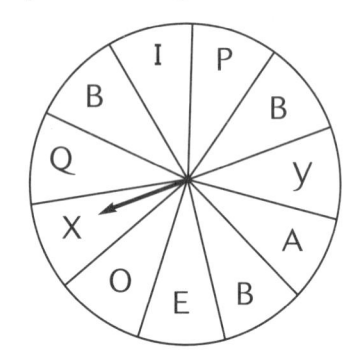

1. P(B or not P)

   A $\frac{9}{10}$

   B $\frac{1}{10}$

   C $\frac{11}{11}$

   D $\frac{10}{11}$

2. P(vowel or Y)

   A $\frac{1}{11}$

   B $\frac{6}{11}$

   C $\frac{5}{6}$

   D $\frac{5}{11}$

3. Find the mutually exclusive events.

   A Vowel or A
   B B or consonant
   C B or not Y
   D I or B

Use the spinner for Questions 4–6.

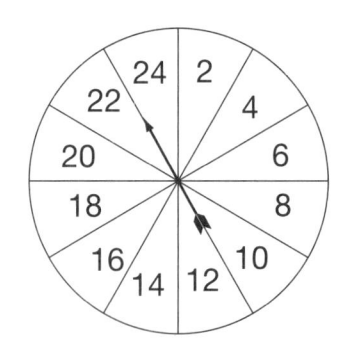

You spin the spinner once.

4. P(2 or multiple of 3)

   A $\frac{3}{12}$ C $\frac{4}{12}$

   B $\frac{1}{4}$ D $\frac{5}{12}$

5. Find the mutually exclusive events.

   A 24 or multiple of 3
   B 6 or number less than 10
   C 10 or 2-digit number
   D multiple of 5 or 22

6. P(number less than 10 or number greater than 20)

   A $\frac{1}{2}$ C $\frac{8}{12}$

   B $\frac{7}{12}$ D $\frac{5}{12}$

84

Independent Events

Circle the correct letter for the answer.

Use the spinners for Questions 1–3.

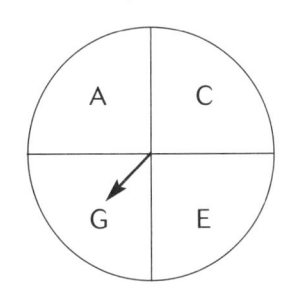

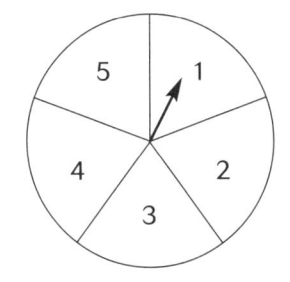

1. $P(A, 4) =$
   A $\frac{1}{40}$
   B $\frac{1}{20}$
   C $\frac{1}{2}$
   D $\frac{1}{4}$

2. $P(\text{vowel, not an even number}) =$
   A $\frac{1}{2}$
   B $\frac{3}{5}$
   C $\frac{1}{6}$
   D $\frac{3}{10}$

3. $P(A, \text{not } 3)$
   A 75%
   B 60%
   C 25%
   D 20%

Use the cards for Questions 4–6.
Players pick a card without looking. They record it, and put it back. They pick another card in the same way.

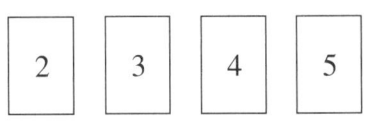

4. $P(\text{odd, odd})$
   A $\frac{9}{49}$ C $\frac{16}{49}$
   B $\frac{12}{49}$ D $\frac{3}{7}$

5. $P(\text{odd, not } 3)$
   A $\frac{3}{49}$ C $\frac{4}{49}$
   B $\frac{18}{49}$ D $\frac{4}{7}$

6. Compare.
   $P(5, \text{not } 5)$ ● $P(\text{odd, odd})$
   A <; because $\frac{6}{49} < \frac{12}{49}$
   B <; because $\frac{1}{7} < \frac{3}{7}$
   C <; because $\frac{1}{7} < \frac{6}{7}$
   D <; because $\frac{6}{49} < \frac{9}{49}$

85

Intervention Practice **L24**

Dependent Events

Circle the correct letter for the answer.

There are 8 green cards, 12 red cards, and 10 blue cards in a jar. Use this information for Questions 1–3.

1. You select one without looking, replace it, and select another one. Find P(red, red).

   A $\frac{2}{5}$

   B $\frac{2}{25}$

   C $\frac{4}{25}$

   D $\frac{4}{5}$

2. You select one without looking, do not replace it, and select another one. Find P(red, blue).

   A $\frac{4}{30}$

   B $\frac{4}{29}$

   C $\frac{3}{5}$

   D $\frac{8}{29}$

3. You select one without looking, replace it, and select another one. Find P(green, red).

   A $\frac{2}{3}$

   B $\frac{8}{25}$

   C $\frac{8}{75}$

   D $\frac{8}{3}$

Use the cards for Questions 4–6.

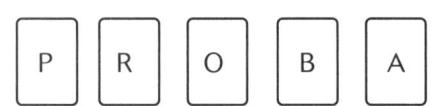

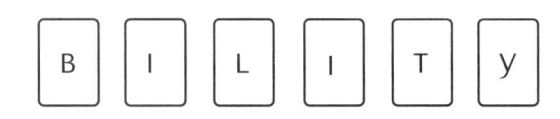

P R O B A

B I L I T y

4. You select one without looking, replace it, and select another one. Find P(P, I).

   A $\frac{2}{121}$ C $\frac{3}{11}$

   B $\frac{2}{11}$ D $\frac{1}{121}$

5. You select one without looking, do not replace it, and select another one. Find P(I, I).

   A $\frac{2}{11}$ C $\frac{1}{10}$

   B $\frac{2}{121}$ D $\frac{1}{55}$

6. You select one without looking, do not replace it, and select another one. Find P(B, I).

   A $\frac{2}{55}$ C $\frac{2}{110}$

   B $\frac{1}{55}$ D $\frac{4}{121}$

Name _____

Intervention Practice **L25**

Making Line Plots

Fill in the ○ for the correct answer.

Use the line plot to answer the questions.

Students Absent from School in One Week

```
X
X                         X
X       X                 X
X       X       X         X
─────────────────────────────
Monday Tuesday Wednesday Thursday Friday
```

Number of Students Absent

1. Which day had no students absent?

   ○ Monday   ○ Wednesday
   ○ Tuesday   ○ Friday

2. How many students were absent on Thursday?

   ○ 1 student   ○ 3 students
   ○ 2 students ○ 4 students

3. How many students were absent on Monday and Tuesday?

   ○ 5 students ○ 7 students
   ○ 6 students ○ 8 students

4. How many students were absent on Wednesday and Thursday?

   ○ 4 students ○ 5 students
   ○ 2 students ○ 7 students

5. On which day were the most students absent?

   Monday   Tuesday   Wednesday   Friday
     ○   ○   ○   ○

87

Intervention Practice L26

Mean, Median, and Mode

Circle the correct letter for the answer.

1. Akins keeps a record of the number of goals he scores at soccer games. Which is the mode for the data?

Goals Scored	
Game 1	1
Game 2	2
Game 3	4
Game 4	1
Game 5	2
Game 6	4
Game 7	1
Game 8	1

A 4
B 3
C 1
D 2

2. Sean was paid the following amounts for doing chores.

$4.00	$4.65	$5.50	$4.85
$3.00	$4.00	$3.75	

Find the median for this set of data.

A $3.00
B $4.00
C $4.25
D $5.50

3. Find the mean for this set of data.

Tree Heights (ft)				
35	53	47	32	53

A 21
B 44
C 47
D 53

The line plot shows the number of minutes Kari waited for a bus on 10 days. Use the line plot for Questions 4–6.

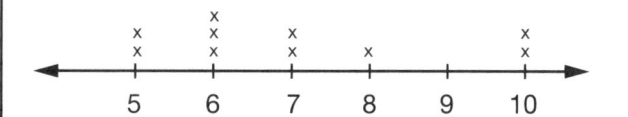

4. Find the median number of minutes she waited.

A 6
B 6.5
C 7
D 7.5

5. Find the mean number of minutes she waited.

A 6
B 6.5
C 7
D 8

6. Find the mode number of minutes she waited.

A 6
B 6.5
C 7
D 5

Intervention Practice **L27**

Finding Averages

Circle the correct letter for the answer.

1. The following represent amounts Thom earned babysitting.

   $17 $20 $17 $33 $22 $23

   What is his mean income?

   A $17
   B $21
   C $22
   D $33

2. What is the mean of bicycle tire sizes: 18 inches, 24 inches, 24 inches, and 26 inches?

   A 18 in.
   B 22 in.
   C 23 in.
   D 24 in.

3. Students in Mr. Ramirez's class read the following number of books during the summer.

   4   6   0   1   0   5   2   14

   What was the mean number of books read?

   A 0
   B 3
   C 4
   D 8

Top 10 Video Game Prices	
1	$39
2	$45
3	$35
4	$59
5	$69
6	$39
7	$49
8	$50
9	$39
10	$59

4. What is the mean price of the video games?

   A $45.00   C $50.00
   B $48.30   D $52.80

5. What is the mean of this set of data? 7, 2, 4, 7, 6, 7, 2

   A 5   C 6
   B 4   D 7

6. Find the mean hourly wage: $6.10, $5.80, $9.50, $10.20, $4.50, $6.40, $5.00, $6.10.

   A $5.80   C $6.70
   B $6.10   D $6.30

89

Name _____

Intervention Practice **L28**

Stem-and-Leaf Plots

Circle the correct letter for the answer.

1. Here are the heights of 10 students, in inches:

   60, 58, 63, 70, 65, 66, 60, 62, 57, 65.

   Which height is missing from the stem-and-leaf plot?

Stem	Leaves
5	7 8
6	0 0 2 3 5 6
7	0

   A 50   **C** 63
   B 62   **D** 65

The stem-and-leaf plot shows football scores for Main School. Use the diagram for Questions 2 and 3.

Stem	Leaves
0	0 2 3 6 7
1	2 2 5 7 8 8
2	0 0 0 1 1 3

2. Find the median of the data.

   A 12   **C** 18
   B 17   **D** 20

3. Find the mode of the data.

   A 12   **C** 18
   B 17   **D** 20

The stem-and-leaf plot shows the results of a crossword puzzle contest at LaCross School.
Use the stem-and-leaf plot for Questions 4–6.

Minutes Needed to Solve a Crossword Puzzle

Stem	Leaves
1	9
2	4 4 5 6 9 9
3	0 0 1 1 1 2 4 4 5 5 5 6 8 8 8
4	1 3 7 8
5	2 3

4. What is the median number of minutes it took to solve the crossword puzzle?

   A 30   **C** 32
   B 31   **D** 34

5. How many people solved the crossword puzzle in less than 20 minutes?

   A 0   **C** 2
   B 1   **D** 3

6. How many people reported they needed 35 minutes to solve the crossword puzzle?

   A 3   **C** 1
   B 2   **D** 0

Name _____

Intervention Practice **L29**

Sampling Methods

Circle the correct letter for the answer.

1. Identify the sampling method: A person asks those entering a mall about their favorite beverage.

    A Random sampling
    B Responses to a survey
    C Convenience sampling
    D Representative sampling

2. Identify the sampling method: The principal chooses every 5th student from an alphabetical list to ask about lunch preferences.

    A Random sampling
    B Responses to a survey
    C Convenience sampling
    D Representative sampling

3. Which sample is likely to be unbiased?

    A Choosing random phone numbers to ask them their preferred cleaning product.
    B Having a candidate ask voters whom they plan to vote for.
    C Asking readers to return a survey about their income.
    D Asking the Spanish club their preferred eating establishment.

4. Identify the sampling method: A magazine asks its readers to return a survey on vacation spots.

    A Random sampling
    B Responses to a survey
    C Convenience sampling
    D Representative sampling

5. Identify the sampling method: Samples from 5 different spots in a pond are taken and studied to determine pond life in that pond.

    A Random sampling
    B Responses to a survey
    C Convenience sampling
    D Representative sampling

6. Which sample is likely to be biased?

    A Asking every 5th person who passes by a street corner about the upcoming election in a town.
    B Asking the girl students to return a survey about their favorite books.
    C Asking each member of the Math Club about his or her preference for an end of the year party.
    D Pulling every 3rd registration sheet to tally the number of siblings in the school.

Frequency Tables and Line Plots

Circle the correct letter for the answer.

1. Given the data set 56, 52, 54, 43, 53, 57, and 56. Which of the numbers is an outlier?

   A 57   **B** 56   **C** 52   **D** 43

2. Which data is shown in the frequency table?

Number	Tally
1		
2			
3				

   A 1 2 2 1 3 3
   B 3 3 2 2 3 3
   C 3 3 3 2 1 2
   D 1 2 2 1 3 2

Use the data set for Questions 3–5.

10   43   43   44   45   45   45   47   48   50

3. Identify the outlier(s).

   A 45   **C** 47, 48
   B 10   **D** 50

4. Calculate how much the outlier or outliers affect the mean.

   A The outliers lower the mean from 45.6 to 42.
   B The outliers lower the mean from 45 to 35.
   C The outliers raise the mean from 41 to 46.
   D The outliers do not affect the mean.

5. How do the outlier or outliers affect the mode?

   A The outliers change the mode from 40 to 45.
   B The outliers raise the mode from 45 to 47.
   C The outliers lower the mode from 45 to 43.
   D The outliers do not change the mode.

Use the line plot for Questions 6–8.

```
    X X
    X X
X X X X                              X   X
6 7 8 9 10 11 12 13 14 15 16 17 18 19
```

6. What is the range of the data set?

   A 25   **C** 13
   B 19   **D** 10

7. Which is the mean of the data, including any outliers?

   A 10   **C** 7
   B 8   **D** 6

8. How do the outlier or outliers affect the mean?

   A The outliers lower the mean by 1.
   B The outliers lower the mean by 2.
   C The outliers raise the mean by 2.
   D The outliers do not affect the mean.

Intervention Practice **L31**

Misleading Graphs

Circle the correct letter for the answer.

Use the line graph for Questions 1–2.

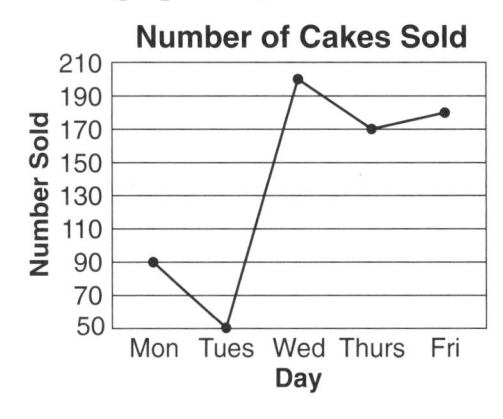

Number of Cakes Sold

1. Which conclusion is correct?

    A The number of cakes sold on Monday is more than twice the number of cakes sold on Tuesday.

    B The total number of cakes sold on Thursday was three times as that on Tuesday.

    C There were no cakes sold on Tuesday.

    D There were almost four times as many cakes sold on Wednesday than on Tuesday.

2. How could you redraw the graph so it appears the same number of cakes were sold each day?

    A Begin the vertical scale at 150.

    B Use units of 10 instead of 20.

    C Use units of 100 instead of 20.

    D Display the data in a circle graph.

Use the bar graph for Questions 3–5.

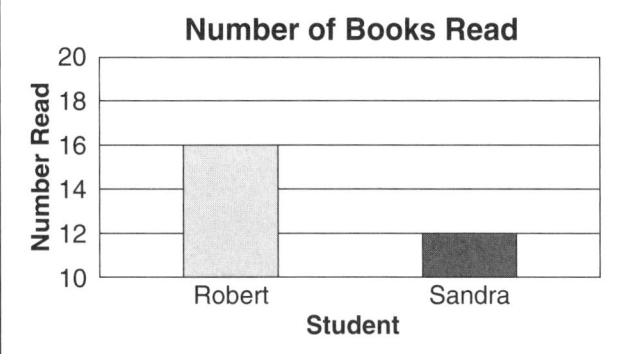

Number of Books Read

3. Which claim is the most accurate?

    A Robert read three times as many books as Sandra.

    B Sandra read more books than Robert.

    C Robert read fewer books than Sandra.

    D Robert read four more books than Sandra.

4. Which is the best way to redraw the graph to show that Robert and Sandra read about the same number of books?

    A Begin the vertical scale at 0.

    B Use units of 1 instead of 2.

    C Make the bars more narrow.

    D Use a line graph.

5. How many books did Robert read?

    A 12   **C** 14

    B 13   **D** 16

93